The Princess of 42nd Street

Surviving My Childhood as the Daughter
of Times Square's KING of PORN

By **ROMOLA HODAS**
WITH ELIZABETH RIDLEY

The Princess of 42nd Street: Surviving My Childhood as the Daughter of Times Square's King of Porn© Romola Hodas 2018

All Rights Reserved. No part of this book may be reproduced or transmitted in any form or by any means, electronic or mechanical, including photocopying, without permission in writing from the publisher.

For more information contact:
Riverdale Avenue Books
5676 Riverdale Avenue
Riverdale, NY 10471

www.riverdaleavebooks.com

Design by www.formatting4U.com
Cover by Scott Carpenter

Digital ISBN: 9781626014725

Print ISBN: 9781626014718

First Edition September 2018

This book is dedicated to my family, whom I love very much, and yes, Mom and Dad, you, too.

I also dedicate this book to the many people who have experienced trauma and abuse—if this book motivates you to choose yourself and to start or restart an important journey, then I am happy, because I have achieved my goal.

"Believe in yourself and all that you are. Know that there is something inside you that is greater than any obstacle." *–Christian D. Larson*

"A journey of a thousand miles begins with a single step." *–Lao Tzu*

DISCLAIMER

The Princess of 42nd Street: Surviving My Childhood as the Daughter of Times Square's King of Porn represents the story of the first 25 years of my life to the best of my recollection. I have recreated events, locations and conversations based on my memories of them. In some instances, I have changed the names of individuals in order to maintain their anonymity. I acknowledge that others, including members of my family, may remember differently some of the events described in this book.

TABLE OF CONTENTS

A Note from the Author		i
Prologue: The Porno King of 42nd Street Expands His Empire (1972)		1
1	The King of Porn is Born (1931-1961	7
2	Hard Punches and Bee Pinches (1962-1965)	14
3	Misery in Malverne (1965)	22
4	A Visit from Grandma's Ghost and the Surprising Fun of Fat Camp (1965-1968)	31
5	The Lord of the Loops Assumes His Throne (1968-1970)	37
6	Fat Camp, Flattened Frogs and Kidnap-Proof Children (1968-1970)	45
7	First Love and Wicked Knuckleballs (1970)	53
8	Sex Parties, Porn Stars and Swimming Pools (1970-1971)	59
9	Hanging with Strippers, Vacationing with the Mob (1971)	67
10	The Feds Close In (1971-1972)	77
11	Moon Landings, Marty Hodas and *The Daily News* (1972)	87
12	Romola Strikes Back (1972-1973)	108
13	Marty Beats the Rap—This Time, At Least (1973)	115
14	The Joyful Relief of Reform School (1974)	121
15	The House Burns Up and Marty Goes Down (1974)	131
16	The Surprising Fun of Prison Camp (1975-1976)	138
17	The King Returns to His Castle (1976-1978)	147
18	The Princess Becomes a Bride, But Finds True Love with Another (1978-1982)	155
19	The King of Porn Passes On (2014)	165
Epilogue: The Princess of 42nd Street: The Journey Continues (2018)		180
Acknowledgments		187
Resources		192
About the Authors		193

A Note From The Author

In his lifetime, Martin Hodas was called many things: The Lord of the Loops, Prince of Peeps, The Merchant of Sleaze, the Porno King of New York City, to name just a few. He called me "imbecile," "moron" or his favorite, "Fat Moley." I just called him "Dad."

What follows is my story about growing up, from the late 1950s to the early 1980s, as the eldest daughter of Times Square's King of Porn. My father, a brilliant and ambitious businessman, was also mean, violent and vindictive. My mother was a hugely gifted artist and musician who was also bipolar and suffered from a severe personality disorder. In her depressive state, she would take to her bed for months at a time, leaving me to struggle as a surrogate parent to my two younger sisters and younger brother.

Mine was a childhood few could imagine: I was nearly kidnapped twice (and my younger brother *was* kidnapped briefly by the mob and returned, at the age of six), repeatedly sent to fat camp, exiled to reform school, saw my dad go to prison three times, and vacationed with a mobster later murdered in a brutal gangland killing. I was beaten by my parents, routinely humiliated, observed porn stars having sex in our backyard swimming pool, befriended strippers who worked for my father and watched a topless waitress breastfeed a kitten during one of my parents' parties.

My story certainly has its darker moments, but you will find humor in these pages too, humor and hope. Hope always burned brightly inside me, even during the darkest of times. I knew from the earliest age that something was very wrong with my parents, and I knew that something would be very wrong with me if I didn't get help, if I didn't learn how to treat myself with kindness, how to "choose" myself and nurture myself in the ways my parents failed to nurture me. I seemed to understand instinctively, even as a very young child, that I would only be Romola Hodas one time, so it was up to me to figure out what brought me happiness and then pursue it.

I waited to publish this story until after both my parents had passed away (Mom in 2004 at age 66 from complications of diabetes; Dad in 2014 from COPD at the age of 82). I knew I couldn't tell this story unless I could tell the truth, the whole truth and nothing but the truth as I recalled it, no matter how raw, brutal or painful that truth might be. But I also knew I couldn't bear to hurt or humiliate my parents. For all the terrible things they did to me and my siblings, I never once stopped loving them. I have also tried my best not to hurt or embarrass my sisters and brother by telling this story, because I love them very much too.

The Princess of 42nd Street is a story about many things: the growth of the pornography and sex industry, the history of Times Square, the story of how Marty Hodas, a scrappy Jewish kid from Brooklyn, parlayed a couple of gumball machines into a multimillion-dollar adult entertainment empire. It is also the story of the lifelong struggle to overcome an abusive childhood and build a healthy adulthood from the wreckage of a shattered past. It is all these things, but mostly, *The Princess of 42nd Street* is a story about forgiveness. My father gave me much to forgive, as did my mother. I loved them both, and I have forgiven them both, not only for their sake, but also for my own. I forgave them so I could be free. And I share this story with you in the spirit of forgiveness.

So, Daddy, whaddya think? Are you proud of your little girl now?

Prologue

The Porno King of 42nd Street Expands His Empire
1972

"Romola, come see me this afternoon. I wanna show you something, at the theater across from my office." My dad slouches beside the kitchen sink, a stocky, sloppy figure clad in garish polyester, guzzling orange juice.

I almost choke on my Corn Flakes. *Seriously? Dad wants* me *to visit him at work? What the hell for?* Visits to Dad's office are unpleasant, but happily, they are also rare. I would do just about anything to avoid going to see my Dad, Marty Hodas, Times Square's "King of Porn," at work.

Once, we were in his office talking, just an ordinary conversation, when suddenly, I heard a rustling noise from beneath his desk. He never even paused, never stopped speaking, as first the bleached-blond head, followed by the scantily clad body, of a young woman popped up from between his knees. She stood and walked around from behind his desk, wiping her mouth with her hand, not even acknowledging me as she left the room. I suppose he had been "interviewing" her for a position as one of his "girls" while simultaneously getting a blow job. That was my dad, a true multitasker. *Freakin' unbelievable.*

And now he wants me to come see him again? I stare at him while he waits for my answer. Dad's about 5'7" and barrel-chested with a broad face and pudgy hands. He's solidly built, thick, not flabby, but he's always bemoaned his weight. At only 41, he's already jowly, with a stiff, bristly walrus mustache, big brown eyes and a large head with a thatch of thick, dark, wavy hair. His clothes are atrocious: cheap, shiny polyester head to toe with tight tan pants, a garish, tan-and-red diamond-patterned shirt and a dark jacket with oversize pockets and wide, pointy lapels. In the inside pocket of his jacket, I can just make out the shadowy outline of the small handgun he withdraws from the kitchen cupboard every morning before catching the 8:20 a.m. into Manhattan. Dad's had enough dealings with the mob to know when he needs protection.

"Well, Romola? Will you stop by this afternoon?"

I can only surmise that Dad, in his own way, is looking for my approval by inviting me to his office. He certainly can't expect that from Mom, a gifted artist and musician whom we don't realize at the time is bipolar and suffering from a severe personality disorder. We know only her terrifying, bellowing rages alternating with periods of total withdrawal when she is bedridden for months on end. At 15 and the eldest of four, I've tried to be a surrogate parent to my younger siblings for years, and maybe Dad is starting to see me as some kind of substitute wife. *Lucky me.*

Dad looks so hopeful as he gulps down the last of his orange juice, rinses out the glass, and hands me a scrap of paper with the address. It is very confusing for me to see how my abuser, my tormentor, actually cares what I think. Life would be so much easier if I could just learn to hate him. But I don't.

"Sure, Dad." I sigh, staring down at the last few limp Corn Flakes circling the cereal bowl. "I'll be there. Wouldn't miss it for the world."

Later that hot, humid afternoon in the summer of 1972, I hop aboard the Long Island Rail Road from our home in Lawrence, part of the affluent Five Towns area of Long Island, and ride 45 minutes into the city, getting off at 34th Street and Eighth Avenue and taking the subway to Times Square. As I rise out of the dark, crowded stairwell and onto the busy street, I am smack-dab in the middle of Dad's universe, the dark kingdom over which he presides. He owns most of the "adult entertainment" establishments from Sixth to Eighth Avenue. Some kids' dads are doctors or lawyers or teachers or bankers; they visit their dads in skyscraper offices, or bright shiny hospitals, or gleaming banks that smell of money, but no, it's my lot in life to be the daughter of Martin J. Hodas, the Lord of the Loops, Prince of the Peep Show, Times Square's Porno King.

Times Square circa 1972 is nothing like what you see today, the cleaned-up, Disney-ified, family-friendly, post-Giuliani playground and paean to capitalism, with its neon lights and massive billboards for the Gap, Old Navy, McDonald's, Bank of America and Cirque du Soleil. No, the Times Square of 1972 that I walk through has been dubbed the "cesspool of filth," a dirty, dingy, despairing nightmare with rundown buildings, crumbling pavement and garbage rotting in the streets. Hustlers hang at every street corner while vacant-eyed junkies shoot up in shadowy doorways and prostitutes in fishnet stockings, stiletto heels and bustiers openly flaunt their wares, leaning into cars over rolled-down windows and giving potential johns an eyeful of their sweaty cleavage.

But the Times Square of 1972 is more than just another decaying urban wasteland, it is also "sin central," a mecca for adult bookstores, sex toy shops, peep shows and theaters advertising XXX features with imaginative titles like *Deep Throat*, *Secret Wet Dreams*, *Erotic Desires Part 3* and *All-Night Orgy*. Nowhere else in this Nixon-era America, with the war in Vietnam trudging toward its tragic end, is sex such an active commodity, so openly advertised, traded, promoted and sold.

Now, you are probably thinking that this environment is hardly the place for a 15 year-old high school sophomore from Long Island, and you are right. But Romola Hodas is tough; she has chutzpah. By this time, I have already survived two attempted kidnappings (one on the way to school at age 12 and one at summer fat camp six months later); my little brother, Jarrett, has also survived one.

So, I walk down 42nd Street with confidence, my head held high, trying my best to ignore the catcalls, lewd comments and thousand-yard stares from seemingly every man I pass. Catching my reflection in dusty storefront windows, I realize they must see me as fresh meat, with my long, ash-blond hair parted down the middle and blown straight and smooth, my fair skin and my blue-gray eyes. I'm 5'3" and curvy, dressed in the hippy-chic style of the day that only rich girls can afford with bell-bottom jeans, a beaded peasant blouse, hoop earrings, necklace, bangles and rings. Nonetheless, I make sure these guys clearly read my body language, which states simply, "Do *not*—I repeat, do *not*—mess with me."

Dad's business, one of a dozen or so he owns, is East Coast Cinematics, Inc., situated on the fourth floor of a nondescript building located at 247 West 42nd Street. Across the street is an old, abandoned off-Broadway theater, which matches the address on the scrap of paper Dad handed me at breakfast.

I cross 42nd Street and enter the rundown theater, which is hot and stuffy and smells heavily of greasepaint, damp fabric and mold. Taking a deep breath, I climb the creaky wooden staircase to the second floor. There Dad, whose face lights up when he catches my eye, greets me. "Romola, just wait 'til you see this!" Sitting on a high stool beside Dad and taking money is Rizzo, the cameraman who I later found out filmed some of Dad's porn movies. Rizzo is a pasty, shriveled guy of about 50, with a sunken chest, a greasy comb-over and a few, mostly rotten teeth. Rizzo sees me and leers, smiling his gaping, hollow grin. My stomach churns and I feel queasy. Dad opens the door and shoves me inside with his parting words: "Romola, I'm gonna make a shitload of money with this!"

Blinking quickly to clear my vision, I step deeper into the humid, dank, musty-smelling theater. There's a simple, raised wooden stage framed by heavy red velvet curtains layered with dust. In front of the stage, the seating area consists of red-velvet-upholstered chairs arranged in a semicircle with about 20 aisles of seats. About half the seats are filled, mostly with middle-aged white men, men with money, men with nice haircuts and expensive clothes. Alongside them are members of the greasy-trench-coat brigade, the dirty old men you might expect to find here. Mercifully, I don't recognize any of these guys from behind, and no one turns to look at me.

I quickly take a seat at the end of an aisle on one of the back rows, as far from the men as possible. A moment later, the lights go down, the stage's front curtains rattle open, and a long metal chain drops from the ceiling, clinking and clanking, link over link, and sways slowly, suspended over the center of the stage. Attached to the bottom of the chain is some kind of harness made up of belts and chains and buckles. The entire audience holds its breath. No one speaks; no one moves. Anticipation fills the air.

Suddenly a young woman, crouched on hands and knees, crawls out from behind the back curtain and toward center stage. Her long, glossy brown hair tumbles forward over her shoulders as she slinks across the wooden platform, boldly, stealthily, like a cougar stalking her prey. She's dressed in a tight, black leather corset and thigh-high black leather boots with stiletto heels. Her mouth is stopped with a bright red ball on straps tied behind her head.

A man's voice begins narrating the show from a fuzzy speaker somewhere above and off-stage, but my head spins; I hear the words but can't follow what he's saying. Suddenly a huge, hulking man emerges from behind the back curtain and strides toward the woman on stage. He's dressed, head to toe, in a one-piece black leather bodysuit that covers him completely, with only holes for his eyes and nose and a round circle for his mouth. His biceps bulge and he carries a long, thin leather whip.

When he reaches the woman on all fours, he raises the whip high in the air, pauses, then brings it down hard and fast, slashing her across the back with a loud *crack*. I wince, feeling her pain. Tossing the whip aside, he grabs the harness with one hand and throttles the woman with the other. *Oh my God*, I think, *he's going to force her into the harness. Oh my God.* I'm sick, I can't breathe, I'm suffocating. I have to get out of here—

Cut to black. All is silent. I am blissfully free.

* * *

I come to when the show is over. The stage is bare and the men in the audience cough, fidget and zip up their flies. Some get up to leave and shuffle past me up the aisle, heads down, not making eye contact. *What the hell just happened?* I didn't faint; I'm still sitting in my seat, just as I was when the show started. I must have blacked out, my mind going dark while my body remained upright.

As the final men leave, I stand and sway, grabbing the chair to steady myself. My stomach roils and my legs quiver like wet noodles. I turn and see Dad, holding court beside the door, bidding his patrons good-bye, accepting handshakes and congratulations and pats on the back like he's just won some fantastic prize. Dad's business empire has progressed steadily from gumball, jukebox, cigarette and vending machine concessions to "peep shows" to pornographic movies, but this represents a brand-new venture for him—a live S&M sex act performed on stage before a captive audience. He's right—this is gonna net him a fortune. He sees me, and a huge smile spreads across his broad face as he beams with pride. *What the hell am I gonna say to him?*

When I reach his side, I slap him awkwardly on the back and pretend to punch his shoulder. "Well, congratulations, Dad. I'm so proud of you." My voice shakes. "You were right—you're gonna make a shitload of money with this."

He rubs his pudgy hands, delighted, as his brown eyes dance. "I know, Romola, I know." He shakes his head. "And this is just the beginning. There's no end to how far I can take this."

My skin crawls and I'm desperate to get out of there. "Right," I say. "Well, good luck with that, Dad. See you later."

I hurry down the narrow staircase, through the door, and back out onto 42nd Street, where at last I can breathe again. I gulp down air in huge lungfuls as I try to clear my head. "Daddy is sick," I tell myself. "That's it; he's just sick. He doesn't fucking get it; he doesn't even know how inappropriate it was to show this to his 15 year-old daughter. The man doesn't have a clue."

Time would prove Dad right; his "live sex shows" became a huge hit with the porn-hungry public and served as another step in his rise from humble beginnings as a child selling magazines and shining shoes to the head of an adult entertainment empire worth a reported 13 million dollars. For Dad, this day was a triumph, but for me, it was just another summer afternoon in my sordid life as the Princess of 42nd Street, the daughter of Marty Hodas, Times Square's King of Porn. Even so, I clung to hope. I never let go of hope. I knew I'd been placed in this life for a reason; I had a purpose so much bigger and better than this, than life as heiress to a porn fortune. But at age 15, I still had a long journey ahead of me, and I was determined to survive long enough to figure out where my true destiny lay.

Chapter One

The King of Porn is Born
1931-1961

Although I spent my entire childhood living with my parents (except for the year, when I was 17, when my parents had me committed to reform school), I know remarkably little about my parents' childhoods or early lives. They never shared much with us, and the little I've been able to glean over the years comes from more distant family members, snippets of remembered conversations or a few old photos—brief, precious glimpses into the lives of the complicated people that made me who I am today.

I know that my father, Martin Joel Hodas, was born on October 12, 1931, on his uncle's farm in Toms River, New Jersey, the second child of a Romanian-Jewish immigrant mother, and a father who had fled the pogroms of Ukraine and settled in the East New York section of Brooklyn.

Like so many poor, immigrant families, Dad's parents fought hard to survive during the Depression, and I'm sure that struggle shaped the type of people they became—hardworking, shrewd and uncompromising. During those lean years of the 1930s, my father's father, Louis Hodas, or "Grampa Lou," sold eggs door to door, and the money they collected went to buy groceries and pay the bills. Grampa Lou said they earned about 12 cents for a dozen eggs, and a 12-dozen crate netted them $1.44.

I only remember going to the New Jersey farm a few times as a child. Even so, it was heaven for a Long Island suburban kid like me, feeding the chickens and ducking into the henhouse to comb the warm, soft straw for eggs. I loved the farm, but there was something spooky, even scary, about Grampa Lou, so I avoided him as much as possible.

He rarely changed his clothes, and he tied his shoes with tape instead of shoelaces. His left eye seemed "pinched," hanging a bit lower than his right eye, making it always look like he was winking. And his thick lower lip protruded noticeably, as if hiding a wad of tobacco.

Grampa Lou and his wife, my Grandma Mina, divorced long before I came along. Grandma Mina, whom I always called "Grams," was born Mina Cruparu in Romania in 1904, and, at age five, fled that nation's brutal pogroms and emigrated to the US with her parents, Abraham and Bertha, and her siblings. They were a family of barrel makers, and when they emigrated, their last name was Americanized from Cruparu to Cooper.

I loved Grams intensely, and she loved me fiercely in return. She had red hair, broad shoulders, a strong jawline, shimmery blue eyes and a wild gypsy spirit. She was a real "character," full of funny sayings such as, "Never kiss a dog on the mouth; you know he licks his tuchus."

Grams lived in Queens when we were growing up, and I have such fond memories of her preparing for our visits by making a circle of pillows on the floor and telling us we'd be "sleeping in a bird's nest" that night. And she always had a huge crock of her delicious flanken soup, with flank meat, split peas, corn, carrots, celery and plenty of dill waiting for us!

In her own way, Grams tried to protect me. She saw how Mom and Dad treated me, how I among all the siblings bore the brunt of their anger and abuse, so she showed me extra love, concern and affection throughout my life. "Just be good, Mola, just be careful," she would warn, wrapping me tightly in her arms and sending me off with a kiss on the cheek at the end of each visit.

Because I loved Grams so much, I ignored the cruel things Mom said about her. For example, Mom said that during the Depression, Grams would sneak out at night when everyone else was sleeping and have sex with men for money so she could feed her children. If this were true, I didn't blame her; instead, I admired her strength and resilience. Dad told me that Grampa Lou was so miserly and mean-spirited that even when times were good, he often made Grams, my dad, and Dad's older sister, Joyce, share a single bowl of soup for supper.

Perhaps it was Grampa Lou's parsimony that sparked Dad's entrepreneurial mindset. Dad started his first business at the tender age of eight, just a feisty little kid hauling a heavy metal shoeshine box around the busy streets of Brooklyn to earn some pocket money. In fact, he often shined the shoes of Louis "Lepke" Buchalter, a famous Jewish mobster who headed the "Murder, Inc." crime syndicate. That would be just the first of Dad's many run-ins with mobsters.

Later, Dad hawked magazines and newspapers outside the Fulton Street El station at rush hour, bringing in a couple extra dollars a week. During the summers, he worked on his uncle's farm in Toms River, loading 100-pound sacks of chicken feed, adding muscle to his short, stocky frame.

Dad's hardscrabble childhood left him ambitious, focused, driven. He saw for himself a future much bigger than hawking papers and lugging chicken feed. After graduating from Franklin K. Lane High School in Queens in 1949, he hoped to attend Cornell University but instead enlisted in the Army, serving a two-year tour of duty overseas in Europe. It was soon after his Army discharge that he met my mother, Paula Sharon Josefsberg, thus initiating a match truly made in hell.

* * *

My mom's family background was quite different from my dad's. Like his family, hers was Jewish, too, but they were more cultured and affluent. My mother's father, Julius, came from Austria. The "berg" in his last name, "Josefsberg," suggests that his family were historically landowners. Julius worked as a caterer after immigrating to America, and they had money. But when the Depression hit, they lost everything and moved from Huntington, Long Island to Brooklyn. I believe that change in status was hard on my mother's mother and she took it out on her family. My maternal grandmother's name was Romola, and I was named after her. She, in turn, had been named after Romola de Pulszky, the Hungarian noblewoman and wife of Vaslav Nijinsky, one of the greatest ballet dancers of all time.

Grandma Romola died before I was born, but Mom said she looked like Glinda, the Good Witch, from *The Wizard of Oz*. Grandma Romola had a lame arm but played the piano very well. Grandpa Julius and Grandma Romola had two daughters—my mother, Paula, who was born in 1937, and her sister, my Aunt Elaine, who was a few years older.

When Mom was ten, her father died of complications from

diabetes. The story goes that, at the funeral, as Grandma Romola gazed down at Julius in his coffin, she said to Paula, "It should be you laying there, not him." So, clearly, this family had some issues.

When the girls were growing up, Aunt Elaine was very pretty and popular, while Mom was quiet, introspective and preternaturally gifted in art and music. She performed a piano recital at Carnegie Hall while still a teen and was good enough to have had a career as a concert pianist. When we were kids, she could mesmerize us with her music. We had a huge, beautiful piano in the living room, and she could play anything, Mozart, Beethoven, you name it. Saint-Saëns's "Danse Macabre"—thrilling, intense, relentless—was a particular favorite. Sometimes neighborhood kids came over just to listen to Mom play, but if anyone made even the slightest noise, Mom would scream, slam the piano lid shut, and storm upstairs to her bedroom, often not emerging again for days. At the time, we didn't understand that she was mentally ill, or how serious her condition was. We just thought she was strange. Strange, hateful and mean.

Mom wasn't just gifted musically, she was also psychic. When Mom was 16, Grandma Romola was hospitalized with cancer, so the girls' maternal grandmother, Lena, was taking care of Mom and Elaine. They had arranged that Mom would play a certain song on the piano at her mother's funeral. One day, out of the blue, Mom suddenly got up, walked to the piano, sat down, and started playing that song. Lena immediately rushed into the room, flustered and extremely upset. "What are you doing?" she yelled at Paula. "You know you aren't supposed to play that song until your mother passes!"

Mom paused only to answer, "She has," and then continued playing. Moments later, the phone rang. It was the hospital calling to say that Mom's mother had just died. This story may sound crazy, but when I was ten, my great-grandmother Lena confirmed to me that the story was true.

After her mother died, Mom moved in with her grandmother and grandfather, and this was where she was sexually assaulted by her grandfather and his brother, her great-uncle. No doubt her bipolar and personality disorder were greatly exacerbated by enduring that kind of abuse while still a teen. When she finally confided in me about the abuse when I was 14, that allowed me to understand some of why she was so brutal to us.

So, when Marty Hodas met Paula Josefsberg, he had no idea what to expect from this broken, gifted, damaged orphan, still just in her teens. And how could he know? They only dated for four weeks before getting married, on the auspicious date of Friday, July 13th, 1956.

I imagine that to Mom, Marty Hodas, six years her senior, represented the chance to break free from her grandfather and great-uncle. Marty, on the other hand, was on the rebound from a love gone sour, thanks to Gramma Mina. The girl's name was Diane, and she was pretty enough to be a pin-up. But she was a shiksa, a non-Jew, and Mina would have none of that. So Dad ended up on a double-date with a new girl, while his friend's date was Mom. At the end of that date, Dad asked Mom for her number, and the rest, as they say, is history.

* * *

When Dad first met Mom, he had been taking classes at New York Community College and driving a taxi to earn some extra money. After they married, they moved to a little apartment where rent was a whopping $40 a month. Realizing he needed better, more reliable income to support his wife and soon-to-be first child, Dad got a job working for a couple of guys in the vending business who put him in charge of a route of gumball machines. Needing some form of transportation, Dad bought an old-fashioned car for $25, the kind with a rumble seat in back. Dad would stack the gumball machines in the rumble seat and drop them off at the candy stores along his route.

The gumball machines only took pennies, but some machines were so popular, Dad had to empty the machines and collect the money twice a week or else the machines got clogged and stopped working. Soon, Dad was making $15 per machine and servicing 40 machines per week, which netted him $600 a week in income. This was a huge amount of money in the late '50s/early '60s, when the average worker's take-home pay was a fraction of that. Dad may not have realized it at the time, but those gumball machines sowed the first tiny seeds of his future adult entertainment empire.

Meanwhile, Dad was planting other seeds as well. My parents had been married less than a year and were living in Kew Gardens, a working-class section of Queens, when I was born on June 9th, 1957, the first of their four children. Mom showed little if any maternal instinct, and motherhood worsened her symptoms of mental illness. What was most painful was how Mom could be so kind and loving one moment, and so cruel the next. On one hand, she would say what a special child I was and call me her beautiful "pink-and-white baby," the only girl born at the hospital that day. But then she would also leave me alone in my crib, in a cold, dark room, for hours and hours unattended as I cried my lungs out. I would cry so hard that I vomited, and then she would scream at me for vomiting and being such a terrible child.

When I was a year old, we moved from Kew Gardens to Bethpage, a blue-collar enclave on Long Island, best known at the time as the headquarters of the Grumman Aircraft Engineering Corporation, the company that produced modules for the Apollo moon landing. Our house in Bethpage was small, cramped and dark, a setting that matched Mom's increasingly black moods. Often she would just sit in the dark, alone, staring into space.

In September 1959, my younger sister Risa was born. Mom also often left Risa alone screaming in her carriage, and although I was only two, I would climb up into the carriage beside her and hold her, kissing and comforting her until she calmed down. Risa was a round, happy baby with pink cheeks and curly red hair. Her ears stuck out a little, and Daddy would later cruelly dub her "Dumbo," but to me, she was perfect and beautiful, like a little doll come to life. As young as I was, I already understood that it was up to me to give Risa the love that neither of us was getting from Mom.

If Mom was my tormentor during my first years of life, Dad was my hero, my savior, the one I looked to for love, acceptance and support. When we lived in Bethpage, our quiet residential street led to a much busier thoroughfare. When I was only about three or four, in the early evening I would sit on the curb where the quiet street met the busy road, watching for Daddy to come home from work. This was the highlight of my day. And imagine, my mother had no clue I was gone, sitting so close to the busy street.

Sometimes I'd be wearing bib overalls, and other times, a frilly pink dress with ruffles. I would push my white-blond curls out of my eyes and peer down the street, watching for my father's long, tan station wagon to come zooming around the corner. As soon as I saw the car, I'd start running toward the house to meet him when he pulled in the driveway.

Out of breath, I'd stand there, panting, fists on hips, just waiting to be loved by Daddy. He'd get out of the car, at age 30 already 200 pounds and barrel-chested, and give me a big, jolly smile that lit up his broad, round face.

"Daddy! Daddy!" I squealed with delight as he picked me up, whisked me high in the air, then caught me safely in his arms as I came sailing back down.

Mom would run out of the house yelling, "Marty! Stop it! You're going to drop her!" but I would think, *Go away, Mom. Leave us alone and just let Daddy love me!*

In those moments, I was the center of my dad's universe, and I felt utterly and completely loved. Perhaps those moments stand out so vividly because they exist in such stark contrast to the violent, vicious brute my father would soon become. Bliss was not yet knowing that in just a few short years, everything would change, and love like this would be nothing more than a distant, bittersweet memory.

Chapter Two

Hard Punches and Bee Pinches
1962-1965

In 1962, when I was five years old, Daddy moved his growing family from Bethpage to Malverne, a quaint little village nicknamed "the Mayberry of Long Island." But in reality, our lives in Malverne bore little resemblance to the homespun rural idylls enjoyed by Andy, Opie, Barney Fife and Aunt Bee in their fictional TV town.

The year before we moved, my youngest sister, Rhonda, had been born, in March of 1961. I was delighted by my new baby sister, who arrived looking like a little Asian baby with pink cheeks; brown, almond-shaped eyes; and a full head of straight, dark hair, so different from the red-haired Risa and me, a golden blonde. Rhonda, who was long and lean until age 12, at first seemed to be Daddy's favorite, and his nickname for her, "Little Fongy," was a term of endearment. But once she was about 12, he turned on her, too, which must have been devastating.

The youngest child and our only brother, Jarrett, a mischievous, pudgy, blue-eyed, blond-haired little boy, arrived in May of 1964, completing the quartet of Hodas children. Unfortunately, having four children did not make Mom happier or more comfortable with motherhood. Instead, Mom's behavior grew more violent, marked by thunderous rages, unprovoked and unpredictable, that were so bad, I was often afraid to breathe in her presence.

She was at her worst when Daddy wasn't home. In the mornings, after he left for work, I would be at the kitchen table trying to feed Risa while Rhonda, strapped into her highchair, played with her food on the plastic tray in front of her. Mom would fly down the stairs into the kitchen, raise her arm, and with a look of sheer hatred on her face, sweep her forearm across the table or counter, crashing everything on it to the floor. Then she would fix her gaze on me, dark eyes blazing, and scream, "Now youuu pick it up!"

My heart pounded and my throat was dry. "No, Mommy, you did it, you pick it up," I'd whisper bravely.

Her cold, hard features twisted into an expression of utter disgust as her eyes stayed locked on mine. "I told you to pick it up! Pick it all up, now, or I will get the wooden spoon!"

Risa cowered in the corner, terrified, while Rhonda, in the highchair, was too young to understand. My deepest instincts told me I had to protect them from our mother.

"You shouldn't hit people, Mommy," I said evenly. "It's wrong." How in the world did I have the strength and courage to stand up to her? I have no idea, and yet somehow, I did.

Furious, Mom grabbed a wooden spoon from the drawer and came at me, raising it high in the air and brandishing it like a weapon.

Steeling myself to take the blow, I said through trembling lips, "If you hit me, I will hit you back." And then, before she could strike me, I wrestled the spoon out of her hand and banged her on the head with it.

"How do you like that?" I asked, breathless. "You don't hit people, Mommy, okay?"

She was so shocked, she retreated to her bedroom and left me alone the rest of the day.

Things were okay for the moment as I finished feeding Risa and Rhonda, but I knew a reckoning was coming, and there'd be hell to pay for what I had done. *I don't care what Daddy does to me,* I'd tell myself, trying to be brave, *as long as I can keep myself and the other kids safe.*

When Daddy came home from work late that afternoon, Mom told him what a horrible child I had been and ordered him to beat me as punishment.

"Paula, c'mon, she's just a kid," Daddy argued. But her stance was fierce and unrelenting. So Daddy gave in and led me upstairs, my knees shaking, and took me to my room, closing the door behind us. I was in sheer terror as I stood before him and watched him unbuckle his wide leather belt with the big metal buckle and slide it slowly through the loops of his waistband. Then, to my shock and relief, he thrashed not me but the bed with the belt. Once, twice, until the bedsprings quivered. "Scream, Romola," he demanded, his voice harsh and low.

What? I was too shocked to respond.

He slashed the mattress once more, harder this time, leaving a slashing dent in the bedspread. "Scream, damn it!" he ordered.

Finally catching on, I screamed bloody murder as the soft mattress absorbed more of the blows intended for me. I began to cry, not out of fear or pain but from relief. I knew I would be fine, even though I would endure similar incidents many times, because Daddy loved me. He was protecting me from Mom. As long as he was on my side, I could endure Mom's hatefulness; I could endure anything, as long as I had Daddy's love.

Daddy was still magical to me then, my hero, my savior, my North Star. So when he promised to teach us how to fly, I believed him. I was around seven at the time and Risa, five. It was right after dinner, and Daddy told Risa and me to lie down and stretch out as far as we could on the floor beside the kitchen table, pressing our knees and chins and bellies to the cool, slick, yellow-and-brown tile. (Rhonda, age three, and Jarrett, still a baby, weren't yet old enough to fly.) I could see Daddy's big feet before me, along with the table's aluminum legs, and, if I looked up, the table's white, oval underside.

Daddy instructed us to lift our arms and legs and practice sailing through the air. I was in heaven. "Move over, Ris!" I bellowed as I spread my wings, "We are going to be flying soon!" Daddy clapped, cheering us on.

After several weeks of flying lessons, one day, out of the blue, Mom must have had enough. Sounding extremely annoyed, she suddenly snapped, "Damn it, Marty, tell them the truth—they are never going to fly."

I was on my belly, swooping over the beach and out toward the sea, preparing to glide in for a perfect landing, when I suddenly dropped my wings, my arms slapping the cold tile. "Daddy, what is she saying?" My voice cracked. He didn't respond and instead simply looked away. I was crushed—*How could he lie to us?* I had worked so hard and waited so long to finally fly for real. I felt heartbroken and disappointed, the way Christian kids must feel when someone bursts the bubble and reveals that Santa Claus isn't real. Mom was so cruel in the way she broke it to us. Why couldn't she have found it in her heart to be kind?

* * *

It was still the early 1960s, a few years before Daddy would assume the throne as Times Square's "King of Porn." His growing business venture had expanded beyond just gumball machines and now included cigarette and pinball machine routes in New York and New Jersey. Some of my happiest times were when Daddy loaded up me and Risa in his big tan station wagon and took us with him on his journey. I was eight years old and Risa was six. I lived for these brief, tantalizing glimpses into Daddy's "other life," the life he lived away from home, and I so loved being able to watch him at work.

Once he'd emptied all the coins from the machines into huge canvas sacks, we'd take the money home and dump the load of quarters onto the kitchen table, the coins pouring forth like liquid silver, dancing and rolling, spinning on their scored edges like ballerinas pirouetting. Then, Mom would help us push those quarters into little cylindrical brown paper sleeves, and we'd tuck in the ends and fold them closed. Each sleeve held 40 quarters—$10 worth of coins. Once all the coins had been sleeved, we'd count the rolls and multiply by ten to figure the day's total haul. Then we'd give the rolls to Daddy to take to the bank. I wasn't sure yet if we were rich, but seeing so many paper sleeves full and round and heavy, stuffed to the edges with quarters, made me feel safe and secure, confident that Daddy would be able to take care of us forever.

Once, when Daddy took me and Risa on his route, we stopped at an old bar in Queens. While he was busy emptying coins from the cigarette machine, I took Risa with me to the ladies' room. Inside we found two nude male mannequins, anatomically correct down to the smallest (and I do mean smallest!) detail. Finding a mannequin in the bathroom was unusual, to be sure, but I was much more curious than shocked. One mannequin had a big red button on the tip of its penis, along with a sign that read, "Don't Touch." Being an inquisitive eight-year-old, of course I couldn't resist. I reached up and pushed the red button. Suddenly, lights started flashing and "BING! BING! BING!" shrieked loudly throughout the building. *OH MY GOD!* I thought. *What have I done?* I knew I couldn't blame it on Risa—she was too small to have reached the red button. Everybody would know it was me.

Luckily, it was still only midafternoon, happy hour hadn't started yet, and only a few of the regulars manned the bar, drinking highballs, smoking cigarettes, and playing pool. When I came out of the bathroom, the bartender was laughing hysterically, the customers were laughing, and even Risa was laughing. But not Daddy—he was livid.

"What the hell did you do, Romola?" he shouted at me, his face red and puffy.

"Sorry, Daddy, I didn't mean to, I-I-just—" My cheeks burned with embarrassment. I wanted to explain what happened; I didn't think I'd done anything wrong. But Daddy stared me down and I was too scared to speak.

"Ah, cool down, Marty." The burly bartender smiled as he polished a glass. "She didn't cause no harm or nuthin'."

Daddy cursed to himself and continued emptying the cigarette machine. The bartender winked at me, then made both me and Risa a Shirley Temple. He must have figured we'd earned it.

The thing was, I couldn't understand why Daddy thought there was something wrong with what I had done when the other men in the bar just found it funny. To me, at that age, a penis was just another body part, no different from an elbow or a kneecap or a thumb. I was still a complete innocent who knew nothing about sex, and I certainly couldn't, at that point, have imagined the role sex would play in my future, and especially in Daddy's future, in his career far beyond gumball, pinball and cigarette vending machines.

* * *

The change in Daddy started innocently enough. When he was watching TV in the evenings on his recliner after work, we kids would play on and around him, crawling all over his arms and legs, making him the center of our games. Sometimes, he pinched us. Playfully at first, but then not so playfully. He began pinching really hard. So hard it left big, round, black-and-blue marks up and down our arms. "Daddy, please be gentler," I begged him.

"These are bee pinches," he explained. But the next time, the pinches were even harder.

"I don't care what they are, please stop, they hurt," I begged. Even Risa would be crying. Then he started grabbing my dolls, especially my beloved Chatty Cathy, ripping her from my arms and punching his fist into her soft stomach and her painted-on smiling face and then laughing about how funny he found it. I looked to Mom for help, but she ignored us, lost in her knitting, with her eyes and mouth so hard and set and angry. She was always so angry, just on the cusp of erupting, even in the quietest moments.

If Daddy doesn't love me anymore, I worried, *who will protect me from Mom?*

* * *

I was still eight when things took another devastating turn. Even at that young age, my body was starting to change, showing the first telltale signs of puberty. It's not unusual for girls of Russian and Eastern European descent to start the process early, rounding out and becoming a bit chubby just before our hormones kick in and womanhood begins in earnest.

The first time it happened came out of the blue. I was in the kitchen, packing up my books for school, when Daddy suddenly glanced over the top of his newspaper and eyed me from head to toe, his lip curling in disgust. "You are so fat!" he shouted. "How can you walk out of the house looking the way you do?"

What?

"You must be the fattest girl in school!"

At first, I was too shocked to respond. "Daddy, I'm not fat," I finally whispered, smoothing down my new pink-and-white flowered dress that had a full skirt and a snug, but not too snug, white belt cinched around the waist. My golden-blond hair was clean and curled, and I thought I looked pretty. I wasn't the fattest girl in my class, much less the whole school. *Why is he saying this to me?*

"DON'T YOU TELL ME YOU ARE NOT THE FATTEST GIRL IN SCHOOL! LOOK AT YOU! LOOK AT YOUR ASS!" Daddy screamed, his face red, his eyes dark and ferocious.

My lower lip trembled as tears welled in my eyes. I tried sucking in my little tummy. "B-b-but, Daddy—"

"Don't you *Daddy* me!" He tossed aside his newspaper, rose from the table, swiped his mouth with the back of his hand, and pointed his finger at me. "You're a fat pig. Don't tell me you're not fat. Your ass is HUGE!"

Grabbing my book bag, I turned and ran out the front door as fast as I could. I didn't start crying until I reached the sidewalk. At eight years old, I didn't know what size an ass should be, and I didn't think mine was bigger than anybody else's. *Why is Daddy doing this to me?*

After that, it only got worse. When Daddy came home from work, the first thing he did was to seek me out. "Romola, where the hell are you? You'd better get over here right now!" he demanded, stomping toward the living room where I sat working on my homework. Hearing his voice, I jumped up and tried to escape to my bedroom, but he was too fast for me.

"No, Daddy, no! Mom, help me!" I pleaded as he lunged toward my arm. But Mom just sat there, passive, detached, not even blinking.

Once Daddy caught me, he bundled me up and carried me under one arm like a squirming sack of potatoes into the kitchen, where he forced me down on the scale that was always stationed right beside the kitchen table. *Who the hell keeps a scale near the kitchen table, anyway?*

If Daddy saw that I had gained any weight—even as little as a quarter of a pound—he would slap me hard and pummel me in the stomach and on the arms. At times, I turned black and blue. All the while, Mom watched from the living room and said nothing as reflected images from the television flickered across her impassive face.

Other times, when Daddy was chasing, berating and beating me, Mom was in the kitchen, preparing dinner, spooning mashed potatoes and peas into a big bowl and carefully placing it on the table alongside a beautiful, succulent pot roast. Still she ignored me, blocking out my screams and my cries for help. Risa watched, wide-eyed, silent as a mouse, hoping that if she were quiet enough, Daddy wouldn't turn his wrath on her. Rhonda and Jarrett were so young, thank God, they seemed oblivious to it. Once dinner was ready, my sisters and brother would sit down at the table and quietly consume everything that was put in front of them, never making so much as a sound.

"You sit right there," Daddy ordered, pointing to my chair. "And don't you dare eat a goddamn thing, you hear me?"

"B-b-but, can't I have something? Please? Just a bite?" I'd ask, tears streaming down my face. "I promise I won't eat much." I was so famished, my stomach kicked and clenched with hunger pangs.

The Princess of 42nd Street

"NO!" he'd scream. "You're too fat. Your ass is too big, and this is what you get for gaining weight."

No one else dared say a word, and I just sat there, weeping silent tears while everyone else finished their meal.

Afterward, Daddy turned to me and said, "All right, you imbecile, clean the table and wash the dishes, then go to your room and finish your homework. This will teach you not to gain any more weight."

Sometimes, after I cleaned the kitchen and went up to my room, Mom and Risa would sneak food up to me. Cold pieces of chicken. Some bread. A few crackers. Whatever they could manage without Daddy seeing them. This was so confusing—*Now Mom's being nice to me? Why?*

I devoured these secret, stolen scraps of food, hoping to fill the gaping hole in the center of my stomach. I was famished, not just for food but for something much bigger—love. Daddy's words haunted me: "How will you ever amount to anything, looking like you do? You can't do anything right, you moron."

And yet, somewhere deep inside my soul, I understood how wrong, sick and misguided he was. This became a major turning point for me. I vowed then that I would never diet, to show him that he should love me as I was. And yet, I always felt fat and was constantly at war in my head as I tried to figure out how to live comfortably in my own body.

My father should love me, no matter what I look like or how much I weigh, I told myself, pounding my fist into my pillow. *A real Daddy loves his little girl, no matter what. Someday, someone will love me the way I deserve to be loved. But it's gonna be up to me to make that happen—I am totally alone now, and only I can help myself.*

Chapter Three

Misery in Malverne
1965

While I struggled at home as "Fat Moley" (my baby brother, Jarrett, called me "Moley" before he could pronounce "Romola," and Daddy actually started calling me "Fat Moley" as a weird term of endearment), my siblings and I were completely unaware of how Daddy's business was growing by leaps and bounds. Still only in his mid-30s, Marty Hodas was well on his way to building the entertainment empire that would ultimately leave him the undisputed "King of Porn."

Nevertheless, he started small. After graduating from high school, Daddy had hoped to study chemistry at Cornell University, but he ended up enrolling in community college to study petroleum engineering after his stint in the army and, after marrying Mom, he got a job servicing gumball machines. From gumball machines, Daddy progressed to jukeboxes. This happened after the two brothers he worked for who owned the gumball machines were unable to pay him, and so they gave him ten jukeboxes in lieu of a paycheck. Daddy saw the potential for building this modest business into something much bigger and grander, something that could support his rapidly growing family.

It might be hard for younger readers to fully grasp how incredibly popular and ubiquitous jukeboxes were from the 1950s through the 1980s. Before our era of Spotify, iTunes, YouTube, and digital downloads, you only had three ways to enjoy recorded music: vinyl albums (LPs), the radio and jukeboxes. The jukebox held dozens of 45s (small records with a single song on each side), usually of the most popular songs of the time, along with some classic tunes. When you wanted to hear a certain song, you would insert your coins into the

The Princess of 42nd Street

machine, punch in the letter/number combination that corresponded to that song, and the song would play. There were large, freestanding machines that played music for the entire venue, and also smaller, table-size models that played songs just for you and your companions while you sat there eating a burger or having a drink.

Jukeboxes could be found everywhere, but especially at bars, taverns, diners, casual restaurants, pool halls, bowling alleys and similar establishments. Because these machines could generate so much quick, easy money, all of it cash, it's no surprise that the Mafia, a very powerful crime syndicate, wanted a piece of the action. By the time Daddy was installing his ten machines, the Mafia, especially New York's so-called "Five Families" (Bonanno, Colombo, Gambino, Genovese and Lucchese), controlled most of the business in coin-operated machines throughout New York and New Jersey. So perhaps it's no surprise that Daddy soon had the first of his many run-ins with the mobsters who, in time, would come to respect and even admire him.

Because jukeboxes were so popular during that era, nearly every establishment that might conceivably have one already *did* have one, so the only way to install your machine was to set yours up in place of someone else's that was already there, an action known as "jumping a spot." Unfortunately, Daddy made the mistake of "jumping a spot" at a diner in Brooklyn, unplugging and pushing aside the existing jukebox to make room for his own. Unbeknownst to Daddy, the jukebox he "jumped" belonged to "Crazy Joe" Gallo, aka "Joe the Blond," a member of the Colombo crime family. In retaliation, Gallo took the spot back, reinstalling his own jukebox and shoving Daddy's in a corner.

Undeterred, the next time Daddy went to collect the money and change the records, he saw Gallo had taken back the spot, so he unplugged Gallo's machine and plugged his own back in. The back-and-forth jukebox war escalated, each jumping the other, until Gallo's machine ended up in pieces at the bottom of a staircase.

Daddy was "advised" by those in the know to sit down with Joey Gallo and work out a truce, but proud, stubborn Daddy wouldn't hear of it. That is, until the afternoon that someone took three shots at him from a passing car while he was driving down the Belt Parkway in Brooklyn. Escaping with nothing more than a flesh wound, Daddy agreed to a supervised meeting with Joey Gallo in Hell's Kitchen.

Daddy, somewhat naïvely, didn't realize that Gallo was part of the Colombo crime family; he assumed Gallo was just some two-bit hood trying to muscle in on his precious territory.

The Hell's Kitchen pow-wow resulted in Gallo securing the jukebox spot at the Brooklyn diner; Daddy's compensation was a mere $50. Even more surprisingly, Daddy and Gallo struck up an unlikely friendship, the low-level mob operative and the future King of Porn, even after Daddy learned the truth about Gallo's mob connections. That's how Daddy was—he judged people by their status in the business world, by how much money they had, by how much he could impress them, and by what they could do that might benefit him.

* * *

As Daddy's jukebox business grew, he used the money generated from those first ten machines to buy and install even more machines, and soon he was running a route of more than 50 jukeboxes and pinball machines all over Brooklyn and Queens. Meanwhile, life at 118 King Street in blue-collar Malverne had some lovely, idyllic moments, when Mom wasn't scary and Daddy wasn't beating me or shaming me about my weight.

I had become fast friends with a little girl named Laurel who lived in the house next door to us. In fact, on the very day we first arrived from Bethpage to view the house, Laurel came over to introduce herself and it was love at first sight. We weren't even five years old but we bonded immediately. Laurel had the entire attic of her parents' tiny house as her bedroom, and the window in her room faced the window in our upstairs hallway just outside my bedroom, so at night we were able to open the windows, lean out and talk to each other over the small sliver of space between our homes. I later developed a crush on her older brother, Wesley, who grew up to be a guitar player for a famous heavy-metal punk band.

Our house in Malverne was bigger and brighter than the one in Bethpage had been, and that seemed to lift everyone's spirits. Still, Mom would often just sit by herself in the dark, and if I asked too many questions, or bothered her in any way, she would lash out, gritting her teeth and demanding to be left alone.

The Princess of 42nd Street

But there were also moments when I saw a different side of my mother, catching fleeting glimpses of the woman locked behind the mental illness. Some days Laurel and Jolene, the little girl who lived in the house on the other side of Laurel's, would come over and Mom would open up her big trunk full of crafts and sit with us for hours, coloring, painting or playing with clay. Mom looked beautiful then, dressed like a cool hippie in her short, crocheted dress with black, knee-high boots and false eyelashes. My friends thought she was so cool, even though they could also see that she was a bit strange. We never knew what to expect with Mom. I remember Risa, barely more than a toddler, asking me, "Who will she be today, the good mommy or the bad mommy?" We lived constantly on edge, knowing she could turn in an instant.

Meanwhile, Dad continued to torment me as well; not just about my weight, but about other things, too. Nothing I did pleased him. I was in third grade when I brought home my first report card with straight A's. I couldn't wait to show Daddy, so as he sat at the table finishing supper, I dropped the card in his lap. "Look, Daddy," I said proudly, brimming with excitement.

As he read the card, his face first flushed and then filled with rage. "Who the hell do you think you are?" he bellowed. "Do you think this makes you better than everyone else?"

"No, I just—"

"Get the hell out of my sight," he seethed, tossing the report card in my face. "Stop thinking that you're something special, because you aren't. You're an idiot, just like your mother."

I felt my heart breaking inside me. I thought he'd be proud of me; I thought he'd be pleased. *This isn't right,* I told myself. *It just isn't right. It isn't how a daddy treats his little girl.*

* * *

Because life *inside* our house could be so miserable at times, I began seeking refuge outdoors. We had a large backyard with swings and a fenced-in area where Daddy kept ducks, frogs and chickens. We also had owls, snakes and a monkey that sat with us at the dinner table and chewed on its tail, along with numerous dogs and cats. We also had pet mice that lived in a big fish tank.

One day, Mom decided she had had enough of the mice, so she stuffed them all into a big brown paper bag and then put the bag into the back seat of the car with me and Risa. She told us we were driving to the pet store to return the mice. On the way there, a cop pulled Mom over, maybe for a busted taillight or something, but when he approached the car and Mom rolled down the window, he peered in, shook his head, and said, "Lady, looks like you've got more problems than just me stopping you." We looked around and saw the mice crawling all over the seats, the doors, the windows. Apparently they had eaten through the paper bag and were making their escape. I have no idea how we got them out of the car!

Overall Mom was pretty indifferent to our crazy menagerie, but Daddy was the complete opposite. He was so caring and protective of all his animals, and I loved that about him, his warm, gentle, sensitive side, even though it confused me. How could he be so kind, so gentle to all these furry, scaly and feathered creatures, but still treat me, his own child, so cruelly? It was impossible to understand, and I sometimes wished he would just be terrible all the time, so I wouldn't have to deal with the pain of hoping he'd show me some love.

That Malverne home remains so vivid in my mind and my imagination; when I close my eyes, I can still see it today as if it were right in front of me. My sisters and I shared an upstairs bedroom that had a bunk bed with a trundle on the bottom. I slept on the top bunk, and when it would thunder and lightning, I would climb down and sit on the trundle, next to the lower bunk, rubbing my sisters' backs, feeling their tiny bodies relax as I vowed to keep them safe.

When I picture walking into that house, I see the green rug with a long gold plastic runner leading to the kitchen table. In summer, we would take that gold runner from the entrance and use it as a Slip-N-Slide. I squirted a trail of dishwashing soap on the runner, then soaped it up with water from the garden hose to make it slippery. It was so much fun, and so dangerous! I don't know how we didn't break our necks.

My parents' tastes were lavish, to say the least, and there was nothing subtle or understated about how they decorated their home. On the right of the runner in the living room were two ornate burnt-orange-and-gold French chairs with a bronze table in the middle. Further to the right was a curved couch, and to the right of that was my mother's beloved piano. Her talent was dazzling; her fingers flew across the keys, bringing Beethoven, Tchaikovsky and Chopin magically to life. Even in Malverne, neighborhood kids came in from playing outside just to listen and sat on our floor, mesmerized. But if you made one too many noises, slam went the piano lid and Mom would storm out, often not speaking to anyone again for days.

Past the white Formica table in the kitchen was the Lay-Z Boy, to the right was Mom's rocking chair, in front of the Lay-Z Boy past the door to the dining room, in the far-left corner was the TV, and in the far-right corner, an L-shaped couch, orange in color and sleek Scandinavian in design.

It was here that I sat on the floor, legs crossed Indian-style, and watched the Beatles during their American debut on *The Ed Sullivan Show,* February 9th, 1964. I cried when their set was over. "Not yet, not yet, Mommy, don't let them be finished!" I begged my mother. I felt a weird sensation watching these four young men. Apparently this was some budding sexual desire welling up inside me, and I wasn't yet seven years old. It was John Lennon's powerful voice, his sensual lips, the way he held his guitar and moved up and down as he sang. How could I have been so young and already falling for the bad boys? And just what did this bode for my future relations with the opposite sex?

TV represented a safe place to get away from the stress and sorrow of my world. We all loved watching *Star Trek* at 6:00, even Mom, and I remember rushing home from school to watch that weird black-and-white vampire soap opera, *Dark Shadows*. On the weekends, the other kids and I would all huddle up in front of the TV and put the volume as low as possible to still be able to hear it as we watched *Davy and Goliath*, the clay animation program. If we were too loud, Mom would fly downstairs, screaming and ready to swing. I would look at her and warn her that if she hit anyone, I would hit her back. As terrified as I was, I just knew this wasn't how most mommies acted, and I knew that none of us deserved to be hit.

In addition to the piano, we also had two pinball machines in our living room, and Daddy kept a working jukebox in our garage, stocked with the best Beatles songs and other favorites such as "I Am a Rock," "Wild Thing," "Baby Love," "The Sound of Silence," "Snoopy and the Red Baron," and "Ballad of the Green Berets." Daddy had rigged it so we didn't have to put any money into the jukebox or pinball machine; we could just play song after song and game after game. The neighborhood kids all loved it, and it felt like half of Malverne came over to our house on the weekends.

The garage door would open early as Daddy headed off to play handball. All our lives Daddy played handball twice a week, claiming that by sweating so much he would leech out all the booze and drugs he consumed during the week and would therefore live a long time. He lived to be 82, so perhaps he was on to something.

Thinking back to that childhood home, my parents' bedroom was upstairs and had a big bed, two windows, and a large dresser. I remember my mother's make-up area and watching myself preening in the mirror, trying on Mom's bra with two rolls of toilet paper stuffed inside to fill out each cup. My mother was a DD. She was so well-endowed, in fact, she would rest her tea cup on her chest after taking a sip. But I also remember, even back then, my mother sitting me down on that big bed and telling me terrible things about my father, including that he hurt her when they were intimate and that he did not know how to play with her breasts. Who in their right mind tells stuff like that to a little girl? Somehow, I knew this was not right, and yet I believed it was my duty, my responsibility, to make things right for my mom, so I always sat and listened.

"Ask him to be softer, Mom," I remember saying. "Just ask him to be nice to you and maybe he will be."

The longer we lived in Malverne, the more Mom and Dad's fighting increased. Often, when he picked on her, she hardly spoke, instead staring mutely, blank-faced, into space. One time, they were sitting at the kitchen table when he started in on her. Suddenly, I couldn't take it any longer, so I grabbed her hand and pulled her away, then stared at Daddy and said, "Stop it! Don't you dare make my mother cry."

They were both stunned. I was stunned, too. How did I go from being afraid of her to protecting her? Afterward I asked her, "Why do you sit there and take it, Mom? Why don't you fight back when Daddy treats you this way?"

She looked up at me, her face dark, her eyes hollow and defeated. "One day you'll understand," she replied, staring off into space.

What? Did she mean that if she fought back, it would be worse? I made a promise to myself that very day. *No, Mom, I will never understand. I will never just sit there and take it.* And to this day, I never have—I have always fought back, no matter what I was facing. I owe my very survival to this fighting spirit. Although it certainly has caused me trouble—just ask my siblings, ex-husbands and friends. Of all my personality traits that I've had to overcome, learning to be calmer and not react too quickly has been the hardest to master.

The more my mother retreated into herself, the more Daddy became vicious, violent and hateful to her, constantly berating her, humiliating her and putting her down. His violent abuse knew no limits, and it wasn't just Mom who paid the price, but my siblings and I, too, were often in the crosshairs of his fury as well, bearing the brunt of his abuse. I felt I had to protect Mom and my siblings because if I didn't, no one else would. I began to act out more and more, talking back to Dad, fighting with him, yelling at him not to hurt Mom or the kids.

The more I fought with him, the meaner and tougher he became, calling me names and accusing me of disrespecting him. *Disrespect him?* How could anyone respect a man who beats, demeans and abuses his terribly ill wife and his innocent young children? Of course I disrespected him! He'd done nothing to earn my respect. And yet, nothing could have prepared me for the day he handed me the following letter, written in his crowded, loopy handwriting.

Dear Romola,
You will always be my daughter. This is a biological fact that cannot be changed. As your father I have fulfilled all of my obligations in accordance with the law. All the other obligations that a father has toward his children are from his desire to do so. In most cases the desire remains lasting, but in many cases, this is not so.

As example of this is when the child loses all respect for her parents. There are very few cases in history where the parent turns on the child. It is always the opposite. There are some parents that can accept all forms of abuse from their children and suffer for it. I am not in this category. I have worked too hard and suffered too long to try and satisfy my entire family and do not take abuse from men who work for me or my competitors and will not from my children.

You have two sisters and a brother who in my estimate are all fine, well-behaved children with the proper amount of common sense to recognize the fact that parents are to be respected. Even if a child believes that a parent is wrong about an incident, this does not give the child the right to inflict a barrage of filth. It is apparent that you do not know any better, and also apparent that you do not care to learn.

At this moment I do not care for you as a person. I am not obligated to do anything I don't want to do for anyone. I hope someday you will change.

Your Father

My heart sank as I read these words, and tears fell to the page, smearing the ink. The devastating effect this letter had on me would last the rest of my life. In fact, in later years, when I mentioned this letter to my father, he denied ever writing it. I could have shown him the letter as proof, but I could never bring myself to do that—I was afraid of how hurt, how devastated he might be, to see what he had written to his own child all those years ago. As happened so often in life, I was putting his feelings, his well being, so far above my own.

Even after receiving that letter, I still loved my father, although I didn't—couldn't—respect him as a person. Sometimes I felt so hurt and angry, I had dreams about pushing him off a cliff. How alone I felt at that moment—not yet ten years old, and hearing my father acknowledge in black and white that he did not love me. My mother was too ill to be a parent, and my younger siblings needed me to protect them. But who would protect Romola? I felt like no one in the world was on my side.

Chapter Four

A Visit from Grandma's Ghost and the Surprising Fun of Fat Camp
1965-1968

It's late at night, a hot, humid, sticky New York summer night at our house in Malverne, and I'm asleep upstairs in my bedroom on the top bunk with my sisters sleeping soundly beneath me, Risa on the bottom bunk and Rhonda curled up in the trundle. I'm around eight; they are six and four. I'm dreaming about John Lennon singing and strumming his guitar, and also dreaming of being thin, thin enough that Daddy will love me just like a good daddy should. Suddenly, a strange noise wakes me. I listen. There it is again—a creaking on the staircase coming closer to our door. I lift my head from the pillow, hold my breath, and really listen. You know how, especially in an old house, you can recognize the sound of your dad's footsteps, and also the different sound of your mom's footsteps—lighter, softer, steadier? Well, these are footsteps I hear, but they don't belong to either of my parents, or to anyone I know, for that matter.

"Mommy?" I call out. No reply. "Daddy?" My voice sounds more hopeful than I feel. I look toward the window in the hallway near the top of the stairs, the one through which I talk to Laurel. And suddenly I see a cloud, a damp, thick, misty cloud that, although nebulous, has form and shape and dimension as it hovers in our doorway. For a moment, I am frozen in fear, and then my hands shake and I almost trip as I climb down the ladder from the top bunk and sit between Risa and Rhonda, putting my hands on their backs as they sleep.

The cloud begins to roll into our room, growing in size and malevolence. I scream. At the top of my lungs, I scream. "Mommy! Daddy! Help!!" No one comes. Risa and Rhonda wake up, terrified.

Mommy and Daddy should be right below us, downstairs watching TV—where are they?

"Help us, please!" I scream again. When still they don't respond, I muster all my courage, take a deep breath, jump off the bed and run out of the bedroom, running straight through the misty cloud, feeling the cold wetness on my face as I race through it. Down the stairs I run, looking everywhere for Mom and Dad, desperate to find them before the cloud captures and consumes my little sisters, and Jarrett, too.

I finally find Mom and Dad outside, where they have taken the little TV from inside and set it up so they can watch it from their lawn chairs. They have never done this before, as far as I know.

"Help! It's going to get them! The cloud is going to get Risa, Rhonda and Jarrett!" I scream. Daddy jumps up first and grabs me, carrying me inside and running up the stairs with Mom close behind. I'm still screaming "It's going to get them" as we rush into the bedroom. The cloud is gone, and Risa and Rhonda are sitting upright in the bed, blinking drowsily and looking confused.

"Go back to sleep," Mom tells us nonchalantly. "That was just my mother coming to look in on you children and say hello. All is well; go back to bed." *What? Grandma Romola, who died when Mom was 16? Now she's visiting us from beyond?!?!*

I look straight into Mom's eyes. She believes this, and more than that, it doesn't bother her at all. She is completely cool, calm and collected as she tucks my sisters back under the covers. Then again, perhaps I shouldn't be surprised, because Mom has always had psychic abilities.

For example, she used to warn me not to ride on the handlebars of my friend Karen's bike, but of course, I didn't listen. One day after school, I was a mile from home, riding on Karen's handlebars, and I fell off, badly cutting my hand. When I got home, I walked in the house and Mom and Vicki, her friend from across the street, were in the living room. Mom was sitting on the couch, smoking a Virginia Slim. Without even turning around to look at me, she said, "Romola, what did I tell you about that bike? Do you see that cut on your hand? You are going to have a scar there for the rest of your life." Sure enough, I am looking at that scar right now, even as I type these words, and it still gives me the chills just to think about it.

* * *

While Mom was getting weirder, Dad was getting richer, and the Hodas family was moving up in the world. Dad now owned 60 jukeboxes and was expanding his business interests beyond just jukebox, pinball and cigarette machines to 25-cent, coin-operated "peep shows," which I will describe in more detail in the next chapter.

As young as I was, I knew little, and understood less, about what my father did for a living. All I knew for sure was that those massive canvas sacks of quarters kept coming home with Daddy, and we were richer than we had ever been before. As a sign of his burgeoning wealth, in 1967, Dad began building a big, new, four-bedroom home with quarters for a live-in maid in Lawrence, part of the affluent Five Towns area on the southern shore of Long Island.

We're getting a live-in maid? I marveled when he told us. *What the hell? Are we moving to Long Island, or Beverly Hills?* Not only that, he had purchased a boat, a 40-foot cabin cruiser that he named "My Three Girls" and docked in Oceanside while we were still living in Malverne waiting for the new house to be finished.

While the new house was being built, he would sail us out there and dock in our soon-to-be new backyard. I would walk up the dock surrounded by the wood pilings, taking long, slow, deep breaths, filling my lungs with the musty, woody smell as the pool and then the house took shape. I was in awe, watching the house come to life in different stages, rising from its foundation like magic; each time we visited, it was a little more complete. The bottom level of the house featured big, beautiful jagged pieces of stone in a variety of colors, tan, light orange, brown, and ivory, while the upper level of the house was constructed of redwood.

As we tramped through the backyard, Daddy would describe for us how the house would look, saying, "This is going to be the pool, and here's where the cabanas will be. Our house is going to be 12 feet longer than any other house on the water in Lawrence Bay Park!"

That was important to Dad; whatever he had, it had to be bigger and longer and more ostentatious than anyone else's. He was so proud, and so excited, just like a little kid. We were excited, too. We'd park ourselves in the unfinished kitchen, where the appliances hadn't yet been installed, and we'd have sandwiches and sodas, sitting cross-legged on what was still a sawdust floor. I felt such hope in those moments. *Lawrence will be different,* I thought. *Mom and Dad will be kinder to us, and they will get along better. Mom will have her own big, sunny studio on the second floor, overlooking the inlet and the Atlantic Beach Bridge. She'll be able to do her artwork, and we'll all be happier. In Lawrence, we'll all have a new start.*

* * *

I didn't know a lot about Lawrence, but I found out soon enough that I would have to look and act a certain way if I wanted to fit in with the rich, thin, beautiful, stylish girls who called the Five Towns home. I was desperate to lose weight, even though I wasn't fat by normal standards. Dad still berated me constantly; on a good day I was "Fat Moley"; on a bad day (and there were lots of bad days), I was a "moron," an "imbecile," "disgusting" and the girl with "the fattest ass in school." Even so, he and Mom refused to help me lose weight. And I knew nothing about dieting, and part of me never wanted to learn. People should like me for me, not my body weight. It was all so confusing.

I knew I had to do something before we moved to Lawrence and I entered a new school. It was the summer of 1968, I had just turned 11, and I'd be starting sixth grade in the fall. When my parents were discussing sending us to summer camp, I gathered up the courage to tell them where I really wanted to go—fat camp. Camp Napanoch, in Ellenville, in the Catskill Mountains of New York, to be precise. To my surprise, Mom and Dad said yes, and decided to send Risa and Rhonda, then ages nine and seven, as well, even though neither one needed to lose weight. I think my parents just wanted us girls out of the way while they completed the move from Malverne to Lawrence.

Camp Napanoch was beautiful, and I ended up loving my time there. Okay, the food was terrible—breakfast could be wet toast with cottage cheese and cinnamon sprinkled on top (to this day, I cannot stand cottage cheese), or oatmeal with a slice of American cheese on top. For example, for lunch, we got two hot dogs with one bun, and as much sauerkraut as we could stomach, or grilled chicken with a wet, wilted tomato draped over it.

What the camp food lacked, however, the camp activities more than made up for. I fell in love with horseback riding, along with swimming, archery and arts and crafts. We even had a field trip to go see the famous rock band The Who play a concert at The Tamarack Lodge on Monday, July 29th. How many kids got to see The Who on stage at age 11? And not only that, but I got to sit in the second row!

For the first time since I was eight years old and Dad started beating me up about my weight, I felt "normal," not a freak, but comfortable in my own skin. I felt at home, surrounded by other kids who were like me, even though I was one of the thinnest kids there. Risa and Rhonda were so homesick the first few weeks, especially Risa, who was terribly shy, but after a while, they adjusted.

In total, we spent two months at camp, and halfway through, after we'd been there about a month, there was a visiting weekend for parents and other family members. Mom and Dad and Jarrett came up then and stayed at The Terrace Motel in Ellenville. It was absolutely magical. I had never seen my parents getting along so well. During this visit, Mom was like a different person, sweet and calm and happy. I allowed myself the fantasy of imagining she'd still be just like this once we were all back home. *Maybe she just needed a break*, I thought. *Maybe being away from us for so long, she missed us and remembered how to be a good mom.*

During the day, Daddy would take us up to the mountain behind the motel to hunt for salamanders, newts and frogs while Mom collected moss for the terrarium. Afterwards, we'd bring the frogs and other critters back to the motel and Daddy would let them loose in the motel's swimming pool. "Won't the chlorine hurt them?" I asked, worried, watching them splish and splash, frantically twirling their legs.

"No, they'll be fine," he reassured me. "These are special frogs. They're used to swimming in pools." I was mortified and worried that all the other guests would hate us for messing up the pool with all kinds of slimy creatures, but Daddy was just so lively and funny and childlike. It made my heart sing to see this side of him, the side that was kind and gentle and loved animals. *Why can't he be like this all the time?* I wondered.

* * *

By the end of camp, I had been there eight weeks and lost 12 or 13 pounds. At only 11 years old, that was a huge amount to lose, and I looked and felt so much slimmer. I couldn't wait to get home and show Mom and Dad. I was sure they'd be proud of me. Risa, Rhonda and I took the bus from camp back to New Jersey, where we were dropped off at a Holiday Inn. Both Mom and Dad were there waiting when we got off the bus and then… nothing. Not one word about how much weight we'd all lost or how great we looked.

It felt as if we'd never been gone at all as Dad gave me a cursory pat on the back in greeting, then pushed me firmly away. Mom sat in the front seat of the car, her face hard and closed, knitting furiously and not talking to anyone. I was utterly crushed. What more could I have done? *Did I not lose enough weight to make Daddy happy? Should I have lost more? Maybe the whole summer has been for nothing. Well,* I tried to console myself, *at least I can start sixth grade at my new school skinnier than I've been. At least that's something, I suppose. It's not love, no, but it's gotta count for something, right?*

Chapter Five

The Lord of the Loops Assumes His Throne
1968-1970

My father, Martin Hodas, wasn't the founder of the 42nd Street porn industry; that center of sin was established long before he was even born. His genius, in the period from the mid-1960s to the 1980s, was in being able to take what was already on offer to the discerning (or not so discerning) customer in Times Square (adult bookstores, skin-flicks, some sex-toy shops) and build it into something much bigger, grander and flashier, more provocative, and especially, more lucrative. Dad's insatiable hunger for money was matched only by the public's insatiable appetite for sex, sex, sex.

Almost every major city in the world boasts its own red-light district, from Hamburg's Reeperbahn to Paris's Pigalle to London's Soho. Even so, New York City's 42nd Street is unique. New York City itself traces its roots back to a time before the birth of The United States of America. In the 17th century, Dutch colonists established a settlement in present-day Manhattan that they dubbed "New Amsterdam." The city grew quickly and soon became a national hub for government, finance, politics and entertainment, a status that remains to this day.

By 1899, the area around Times Square had become a hugely successful theater district that was known and respected the world over. The shows produced at these theaters ran the gamut from serious, classical theater à al Shakespeare and Chekov and featuring the top actors of the day, to popular entertainment such as Ziegfeld's Follies and similar musical revues performed by long-legged dancing girls, high-kicking it in risqué (at least for the era) costumes. Female flesh was firmly on display, but overall the shows remained fairly tame, even family-friendly.

After the stock market crash in 1929, The Great Depression

followed, devastating much of America, and New York in particular. "Respectable" theaters such as The Apollo, The Lyric, The Liberty and The Empire were gone, replaced by burlesque theaters, with performances designed to appeal to a slightly less classy clientele. Burlesque, though intended to excite and titillate the audience, never crossed the line into porn. Think more in terms of Gypsy Rose Lee, of *Gypsy* fame, performing a slow-motion striptease to a booming orchestral score, and you get the idea.

The burlesque era, though colorful, was also short-lived. In the early 1940s, New York mayor Fiorello LaGuardia, in an effort to clean up the city, cracked down on the burlesque houses, forcing them out of business. In their place rose up the even-sleazier "grinders," movie theaters that showed second- and third-run feature films (think B-films, and below) all hours of the day and night. Meanwhile, the rest of the area in and around Times Square had fallen further and further into ruin, becoming a filth-infested cesspool of drugs, gangs, crime and prostitution.

The downward slide of 42nd Street's fortunes continued from the early 1940s into the early 1950s, but when Robert F. Wagner, Jr. was elected mayor of New York in 1953, he made it his mission to clean up New York, starting with Times Square. In 1954, Wagner spearheaded a campaign to remove from bookstores and newsstands across the city, "all publications teaching lust, violence, perverted sex attitudes and disregard for law and order." A tall task indeed! Wagner's attempts at a clean-up were only marginally successful, but the seed of righteous change had been sown.

More than a decade later, the push to rid Times Square of its sexual filth was re-ignited when Wagner's successor, liberal Republican John Lindsay, was sworn in as New York City's new mayor on New Year's Day, 1966. Lindsay's tenure as mayor, which ran from 1966 to the end of 1973, coincided with the rise of Martin Hodas' adult entertainment empire, and Dad, never one to shun the spotlight, became Public Enemy Number One, the pudgy, audacious, pugnacious public face of the sex and porn industry, which placed Dad squarely in the crosshairs of the mayor, the police, the Mafia, the vice squad, and all the other forces that had a vested interest in bringing him down.

* * *

The Princess of 42nd Street

Martin Hodas didn't invent the "peep show" machine. The machines had been around for decades, and indeed, by the mid-60s, they were common in arcades in and around Times Square. These peep show machines were hardly elegant or sophisticated devices. The machine itself was a freestanding metal booth about the size of a refrigerator. A guy would drop his quarter in the slot and the little screen in front of him would flicker to life, showing a short, 16-millimeter filmstrip (also known as a "loop") that might be a Popeye cartoon, or a few live-action scenes of Annie Oakley or cowboy Tom Mix. Dad's stroke of genius was loading these machines not with cartoons or popular entertainment but with "girlie films," usually of a buxom woman slowly undressing, stripping down to her underwear.

These films were tame, even by the day's standards, since showing full-on nudity was still illegal. The "aha" moment for Dad came in 1966, when he was driving through New Jersey. He stopped at a roadside arcade on one of his routes and saw a bunch of peep-show machines lying dormant in a basement. And a lightbulb in his head went off. He suddenly thought, "Wow! If I could load these machines with girlie films and install them inside the adult bookstores around Times Square rather than just in the arcades, I could make a shitload of money!"

Dad went back to 42nd Street and schlepped around to all the adult bookstores, explaining his idea about installing the peep machines and offering to split the revenue 50/50. "Sure, Marty," everybody told him, "that's a great idea. But it will never work. Other guys have tried and failed. You need a license—an exhibitor's license, like a movie theater has—in order to run the filmstrips in a machine in a bookstore. And the city will not grant you the license. Don'tcha think, if this were doable, some schlump would'da already done it?"

Dad, being Dad, was undaunted. He talked to Charlie, his lawyer, and they made a claim that not allowing the peep machines in bookstores infringed on their First Amendment right to free speech. The authorities ultimately agreed and Dad secured a letter from the commissioner of the New York Department of Licenses in mid-1967 attesting that a license was not required to "install in the New York City area a coin-operated machine that shows movies."

Dad thought he was on his way! He went back to the arcade in New Jersey and for $2500 bought all 15 of the guy's machines and hauled them back to New York, where he loaded them with 16mm loops that were risqué but displayed no nudity. With the letter from the commissioner in hand, Dad went back to the 42nd Street bookstores hoping to install his machines and start generating some serious money.

But the bookstores still wouldn't bite. Because it hadn't been done before, no one wanted to take the chance that the cops would still bust them for not having an exhibitor's license, the letter from the commissioner notwithstanding. But Dad refused to give up. Finally, his persistence paid off when Hymen Cohen of Carpel Books at 259 West 42nd Street agreed to let Marty install four of the machines in his bookstore.

That very first night after installing the machines, Dad got a call to come down to the store right away. "You gotta see this," he was told. When Dad got there, he witnessed lines that went out the door and spilled over into the street. Dad claimed that there must have been 200 guys waiting to use the machines, although knowing Dad, there were probably only 75 guys waiting. "I think I got something here," Dad told himself. "It's like I invented sex or something!"

Word quickly spread and soon every adult bookstore in Times Square wanted Dad's peep show machines. He had to go empty the machines of quarters three times a week because the machines were filling up so fast they stopped working as the slots clogged with coins and overflowed. Soon, Dad claimed he was bringing in $5,000 or more a week in quarters. It took far too much time and effort to count all those quarters, so he took to weighing them on a scale, taking half for himself and leaving the other half with the bookstore owner. At one point, it was estimated that 85 percent of all the quarters deposited at The Chemical Bank (one of New York's main banks at the time) came from Dad's peep show machines.

Marty Hodas was on a roll, and the money was rolling in. Demand far exceeded supply insofar as every adult bookstore on 42nd Street now wanted the machines, not just because of the revenue that the machines themselves generated, but because of the additional business and sales brought in by the increased traffic to the store. Guys came in to see the peeps, but, once there, they bought plenty of other stuff as well.

The problem was, Dad still only had the original 15 machines he had bought in New Jersey. Dad phoned the machines' manufacturer

The Princess of 42nd Street

in Kentucky to order more machines but was told there was so little demand for the machines nationwide that they had stopped making them. Dad drove down to Kentucky to visit the guy in person and convinced him to build 50 new machines, for which Dad paid $350 each. The production line kicked back into gear, and as fast as the manufacturer could make them, Dad snapped them up, drove them back to New York, and installed them throughout Times Square.

By 1969, Dad had gone from his original 15 peep show machines to more than 300 in 30 locations throughout New York and in four towns in Pennsylvania. Some guys might have been satisfied at that point to rest on their laurels, just sit back and count the money as it poured in, but not Dad. For Dad, no amount of success was enough, and he continued looking for ways to extend his business in new, exciting and even more lucrative directions.

His next venture was the 42nd Street Photo Studio, where he set up a business allowing men to come in and take pictures of nubile young women in compromising positions, often posing with provocative props. This is another example of Dad's brilliant business acumen in action: in those days, it was still illegal to show naked women on film if the film or image would be distributed in any way. But, it *was* legal to take a photo of a naked woman, as long as the photo was limited to "personal use."

So, Dad wriggled around the law by charging patrons ten dollars to spend 30 minutes with a lovely lady in a private room, with the use of a Polaroid camera generously included. Sex wasn't explicitly part of the deal—Dad was trying to stay above the law, after all—but if both parties were willing, who could say what did or did not take place in that private room between consenting adults?

Meanwhile, Dad was having a hard time finding enough films to fill all his peep show machines. The films were fragile, and they broke or split easily, creating the need to order and purchase more films. To remedy this, Dad began producing his own 15-minute sex films through another one of his businesses, Dynamite Films. It took one hour to produce one "loop," and he and his team could churn out five loops a day.

And here's where Dad's remarkable insight, cleverness and resourcefulness again came into play. He wondered which, out of all the various types of sex loops, were the most popular among patrons. So he looked to see which films had generated the most quarters. The most popular, hands-down, were the films that featured lesbian sex. Apparently, guys were super-hot for some girl-on-girl action. The second-most popular films were those that showed plenty of huge boobs. Knowing this, Dad made sure his films included lots of big boobs and lesbian sex. The patrons went wild and just could not get enough.

Now, not only could Dad show his own films in the peep machines he owned, he could also sell these films to his clients directly, in person and via mail order, thereby greatly increasing his revenue. He also started a business to repair the peep show machines when they broke, which they did, often, because of overuse. Dad understood and successfully implemented "vertical integration" of business long before the term was coined (no pun intended).

Perhaps inevitably, Dad's burgeoning success again put him in direct conflict with New York's powerful mob families, who owned a number of the adult bookstores on 42nd Street and who did not appreciate Dad cutting into their profits. Apparently, Dad hadn't learned his lesson after his "jukebox war" with Colombo family operative Crazy Joe Gallo a few years earlier. Perhaps he was naïve, but Dad really believed he could deal with the Mafia on his own terms and still emerge unscathed. The mob thought otherwise, and they let him know, in no uncertain terms.

It began with my baby brother, Jarrett, who was only six at the time and in preschool. A couple of thugs kidnapped Jarrett, picking him up on his way home from the school bus. They didn't hurt him; in fact, the worst they did was take him out for ice cream. After ice cream, they dropped him off safe and sound at our house and sped away before anyone had a chance to identify them. Pinned to Jarrett's ice-cream-stained shirt was a handwritten note to Daddy: *Hi Marty, just to let you know we're thinking very seriously of you.* Apparently, Dad had gotten too powerful, too headstrong, too independent, and the mobsters wanted to remind him who was really in control.

Jarrett seemed remarkably nonplussed by his brush with the wise guys, sitting on the couch in our den and smiling his adorable smile, telling us all about his adventure, but Mom was a wreck, yelling and screaming at Dad, shaking the handwritten note in his face. "What the hell is going on, Marty?" she demanded. "What do these guys want?"

"Don't worry about it, Paula," Dad said. "I know these guys; it's just a message; it's no big deal."

"No big deal?" Mom screamed. "What the hell is wrong with you? This is your son! Those animals took your son!"

Dad refused to get upset, acting like nothing was wrong. The more Mom raged, the calmer he seemed to be. Whether that was bravado on his part, or if he really still believed he could handle the Mafia, I couldn't tell. But for me, this incident was a turning point in my own awareness of who my Dad was and what exactly it was that he did for a living. *My Dad is not like other dads*, I thought. *He does dangerous things, and associates with dangerous people. We are all at risk now.*

* * *

Even after taking Jarrett, the mob wasn't done with Daddy. Or, maybe Daddy just wasn't listening, because the next message they sent him had me smack-dab at its center.

It was the spring of 1970 and I was 12, almost 13, and in the seventh grade at Lawrence Junior High. I was walking to school by myself one morning, down Lawrence Avenue, the long thoroughfare that went, without a break, from our development of luxury houses all the way to the school. With my purse over my shoulder and my textbooks in hand, I was wondering if I had studied hard enough for the third-period algebra quiz, when I saw, out of the corner of my eye, a car, hugging the curb and creeping up very slowly behind me on my right side. At first, I ignored it, just waiting for it to pass. But it didn't pass me. Instead, it followed me. *What the fuck is this*? I wondered. I threw back my shoulders, stood a little taller, and walked with purpose and a swagger in my step.

But then the car came up right beside me and I turned my head. I could see now that the car was actually a long black limo with tinted windows, driving with the back door open. Once the car reached me, it kept pace with my steps, speeding up when I walked faster and slowing when I slowed. Inside the car were three men—a driver in the front, two passengers in the back—wearing black suits and black sunglasses, even though the day was overcast. The passenger kept the back door propped open as he showed me what he held in his lap—a doll. A plastic baby doll, the kind a four- or five-year-old might have. *What the fuck? Does this guy think I still play with dolls?!?*

"Hey, Romola," the big, burly, black-suited passenger called out in a deep, gruff voice. "Come over here. Your mom told us to come pick you up."

That stopped me in my tracks. The limo abruptly stopped, too. "My mother told you what?" I shouted at him. "You think I would go with you and miss school? It's 8:00 in the damn morning. There's no way my mother told you that!"

"Come with us now, Romola. Your mother asked us to pick you up," he insisted, his voice cool and calm. The limo idled in the street, belching smoke from its exhaust pipe as other cars honked and swerved around it.

"I am not coming with you," I announced, "And I'm almost 13—I don't play with *dolls* anymore." Then I stomped off, continuing on my way to school. The men in the limo followed me for a while longer but I ignored them, refusing to turn around, until finally we reached an intersection and they turned the corner, peeling away in the other direction.

Those guys are so stupid, I thought, and laughed. I actually laughed. *What fucking idiots. Maybe if they had come after school, that would have made more sense, but in the morning? No way!* I was more angry than scared, angry that these men dared to think that I still played with dolls, at my age!

Looking back now, I think I was more angry than scared because living with my parents had made me react to fear with anger. Fear was my constant; I lived with it every day. I was like a soldier, a battle-scarred, battle-hardened warrior who used anger and rage as my shield, my armor against a violent and chaotic world. Being afraid meant being vulnerable, and that was one thing I could never afford to be. Being angry was so much easier, and so much safer.

Believe it or not, I never told my parents about my close call with the lowlifes in the limo. I didn't want to scare them—I saw how Mom reacted after Jarrett was taken; she was a wreck for weeks, and I didn't want her to get so fucked up again. In any event, another opportunity for escape would present itself soon, because in just a few months, I'd be spending my third summer at fat camp, and this time, the mobsters would make another, scarier attempt at kidnapping me and sending Daddy a clear, unambiguous message, a message stating in no uncertain terms that Marty Hodas better start playing ball, or else.

Chapter Six

Fat Camp, Flattened Frogs, and Kidnap-Proof Children
1968-1970

The year 1968 was probably the scariest, craziest, most chaotic year ever, or at least the scariest, craziest, and most chaotic year any of us will ever remember, from the Prague Spring and the Tet Offensive to the rising death toll in Vietnam to the assassinations of Dr. Martin Luther King, Jr. and Bobby Kennedy, to the violent, late-summer riots that tore Chicago apart during the Democratic National Convention, transforming the City of the Big Shoulders into a near-police state.

American society may have appeared at a tipping point that hot, desperate, late-60s summer, teetering on the verge of total collapse, but I was feeling surprisingly good. It was August and I was 11, just home from the first of my three summers at fat camp, 12-plus pounds lighter and brimming with hope. While my sisters and I were sweating and starving ourselves skinny at Camp Napanoch in the Catskills, our parents had completed the move from Malverne to our mini-mansion in Lawrence, and I was about to see my brand-new bedroom for the very first time.

The men had just finished their work and when they went to inform Mom, I tiptoed down the hall to sneak a peek. I really wanted to see it on my own, before Mom got there. She had spent weeks getting it ready while I was at camp, designing and decorating the room, and I couldn't wait to see it. Mom was such a gifted and ambitious artist, painting in watercolors, acrylic and oil, and sculpting in soapstone, marble and clay, creating beautiful, detailed pieces rich with vibrant energy, color and movement. I was so excited to see what she had done, but I was also... nervous. Worried, even. *What if I hate it?* She had never asked my input on anything—"Do you like this wallpaper or that one? What type of bed would you like?"—even though at age 11, I already had strong preferences and opinions on everything.

Gripping the doorknob with my hand, I took a deep breath, opened the door, stepped inside and… my heart tumbled straight to the floor. *Oh no. No, no, no.* I wanted to cry. *I can't believe this. I think I'm gonna throw up.* The room looked like it had been decorated by psychedelic leprechauns on a bad acid trip. The wallpaper was a light lime-green covered with small paisley swirls in hot pink, orange and yellow. The shag carpet was hot pink and orange. All the furniture was painted green, as was the daybed. *A daybed? I have to take the bed apart every night before I go to sleep? Shit. Fuck. Damn.* It was clear more than ever that I was a total stranger to my mother, and she really didn't know me at all.

I didn't want her to see my disappointment, so I quickly shut the door and hurried down the hall as I heard Mom coming up the stairs. As I entered the bedroom for the second time, pretending it was the first, only now with Mom at my side, I ohhhed and ahhhed. "Oh Mom, it's beautiful!" I marveled. "I just love it. Thank you so much!" She smiled, a rare smile lighting up her face, firing her deep green eyes.

Later I realized that not only did I not want to disappoint or hurt Mom by being honest, I was afraid that if I told her the truth, she would have another one of her many depressive attacks and end up in bed for a week. At only 11, I felt so responsible for her—for her health, her well being, her feelings. I swallowed my own emotions and hid my true self in order to protect my brittle, fragile, damaged mother. This was death by a thousand daily heartbreaks—child abuse can be so much more than just violence and beatings.

* * *

Disgusting bedroom décor notwithstanding, the first few years in Lawrence were a strange adventure. When the house was still new, I would take my little portable record player and creep down the stairs into the damp, still-unfinished basement, where I would blast the music, shine the floor lamp on me, and dance like a madwoman, casting my shadow against the wall, watching the strange, elongated shapes rise and fall, shimmying against that cold, dark, wet, empty space. The smell of new wood and wet cement was heavenly, and I loved to fill my lungs with it, breathing deeply, drawing it down into my soul. I was aware of being lonely then, feeling all alone in the world.

Adjusting to the new, affluent lifestyle of Five Towns could be confusing. There were some crazy, craven, seriously materialistic people around those parts. We had just settled into 37 Harborview West in Lawrence when a neighbor girl, a girl I thought was my new friend, took me up to her bedroom, played the song "Honey" by Bobby Goldsboro and told me that he was her uncle. *Okay! How cool for you!* Then she told the other kids at school about it and they made fun of me for believing her. What the hell? If my Dad was the King of Porn and Lord of the Loops, why couldn't her uncle be Bobby Goldsboro? Why shouldn't I believe her? It didn't seem so outlandish to me. I had no idea she was just a horrible, mean, spoiled little bitch. This was all I needed—starting sixth grade in a new school and already a laughingstock. I was "Fat Moley" at home and now I was the stupid girl at school.

Around that same time, I was at the grocery store with Mom, and two girls, my age, were behind us in the checkout line. They were both wearing a "chubby," a short, long-sleeved coat made of real fur, either rabbit or raccoon, that was popular at the time. I couldn't help but listen in on their conversation. "My daddy drives a Mercedes; what does your dad drive?" "Oh, my dad's car is much better than your dad's—he drives a Cadillac XL AND a Porsche."

Who the hell cares? I thought. My parents were richer than probably anyone else in the neighborhood, but I saw no need to brag. *You didn't make the money; your parents did. It has nothing to do with you, and you both sound like morons.*

Still, I could deal with morons, and issues at school, and annoying girls from the neighborhood because, for the first time since forever, my parents actually seemed happy. The big new house seemed to give Mom a fresh start, just like I had hoped it would. Suddenly she was fun and bubbly, throwing herself into artwork and decorating. At times, she could be so sweet, offering tantalizing glimpses of the mom she might have been were it not for the corrosive effects of the mental illness that blighted her life.

Sometimes she would get all four of us kids out of bed at 2:00 or 3:00 in the morning saying, "C'mon, get up, there's a great big storm coming in!" and then lead us to her big, beautiful studio on the second floor of the house, with enormous windows overlooking the inlet and the Atlantic Beach Bridge in the distance. We would sit there all groggy and sleep-softened, huddled under blankets, watching massive thunderheads roll across the low, black sky, broken up by dramatic flashes of lightning that arced like arrows slicing toward the water.

Other times, Mom would try to include me as she lay in bed and told me about the stories she was reading, and I would pretend to be so interested, hanging on every word, encouraging her to tell me more. I knew it was her way of trying to be close to me. We had such a strained, and strange, relationship. On one hand, I had been fighting with Dad, begging him to be kinder to her, since I was six years old, trying to protect her from his rages, but then on the other hand, I would be fighting with her to leave me alone and doing my best to stop her from hurting the other kids. It was so confusing, which was why I clung to these rare, precious, tender moments of happiness in Lawrence, hoping they were signs of better times to come.

During those blissful early days, when Mom and Dad were still having fun decorating the house, meeting new people, and getting into their new (and much wealthier) lifestyle, Wednesday nights were their party nights. Mom would put on one of her sheer, lacy, revealing peignoirs that she bought from Frederick's of Hollywood, along with fluffy, high-heeled slippers, her Barbara Eden blond wig, and false eyelashes. She was stunning, and she seemed to feel so comfortable being sexy.

When I close my eyes, I can still picture my parents in the amazing den in the house in Lawrence, complete with a huge bar that was edged with leather to make it more comfortable to lean against. There was a big fake tree in the corner of the bar that tilted a little, and the wall behind the bar was smoky glass that softened everyone's reflection. One wall featured a fireplace that was made of the same stone that our house was made of. On the left side of the fireplace were three animal prints that Mom had painted, and on the right side were six stools that lined the bar.

On their party nights, Mom and Dad liked to indulge in vodka and caviar and play Scrabble. (Yep, the Porno King and his good lady wife *loved* playing Scrabble. It's not like *everything* they did had to be kinky...) If Mom won, she got a gift. If Dad won... well, I can imagine what "gift" he requested Mom give him. Sometimes, before they started playing, Mom would call me downstairs and let me have some vodka and caviar with them before I went to bed. I loved looking at her then, my happy, sexy, confident, pretty Mom; a mom any child would be proud to have. While Mom and I talked and I indulged in these secret, mysterious, grown-up flavors of alcohol and fish eggs, Dad would be in a calm, relaxed mood, having had his standard couple of vodkas on ice, carefully setting up the Scrabble board and stacking the wooden letter tiles.

Dad was a first-class drinker, never happier than when he had a glass in his hand. In fact, the very first time he told me he loved me was during one of these game nights, when he was good and buzzed. And I don't think he ever told me he loved me again, until three days before he died in 2014. God, I still miss those party nights, and those brief moments of feeling so special, so cherished and loved.

* * *

During those years, my relationship with Dad continued on its up-and-down-but-mostly-down trajectory. At times, I loved him so fiercely, it made my heart ache; it took my breath away. He was still magic, in my eyes.

When we came home from fat camp, Dad took the frogs that we had caught and put them in our terrarium. One weekend, Risa and I were riding our bikes and we had a couple of frogs, just little ones, in the baskets on the fronts of our bikes. As I paddled madly, my frog jumped out of the basket and right into my path. Unable to swerve or stop so quickly, I ran him over.

I felt sick as I stopped, hopped off the bike, and bent down to take a look at him. He was flat, lifeless, completely squashed. Horrified, I scooped up the squished frog in my hand and we cycled home to Daddy as fast as we could. If anyone could fix him, it was Daddy. He'd always done magic, going back to when we lived in Malverne and he would perform card and coin tricks for us and for the neighbor kids.

Once home, Risa and I ran inside, crying hysterically. "Daddy, my frog is dead," I sobbed. "I killed him—can you fix him and make him better?"

And to this day, I can't explain how he did it, but Dad took my flattened, lifeless little frog, draped a towel over it, made some pointed gestures and offered up a few words, and lo and behold, when he whisked the towel away, my little frog was alive in his hand, blinking and moving, stretching his tiny legs!

All I can figure now is that maybe the frog was only stunned, knocked unconscious after I ran him over. Or did Dad happen to be hiding another small frog somewhere? In any event, he would never (in the tradition of the best prestidigitators) reveal his secret. All I know is that, even today, almost 50 years later, I still love frogs, and Risa and I still wonder how the hell Dad did that.

But as magical as my dad could be, he never fully left his hateful moments behind. My weight, especially, continued to be an issue with him, even after I slimmed down at fat camp and was well within normal range.

"How can you go to school like that?" he berated me. "You are so fat. Your ass is huge."

"So then stop feeding us so much shit," I shot back. "You send us to fat camp and then we come home and you and Mom are feeding us the same damn crap as before. It makes no sense."

In Lawrence, Dad had started holding monthly card games with his buddies, and he stocked the cupboards with all kinds of shitty junk food for him and his pals—candy bars, soda, pretzels, Snickers, M&Ms, potato chips, you name it, all the things I liked best, just spilling off the shelves, enticing me with their shiny, brightly colored wrappers.

"Daddy, can't you just lock all that junk food away in the safe until your party, so I don't have to see it every day?" I pleaded with him. "That would really help me lose weight like you want me to."

"What, are you KIDDING ME?" he screamed in my face. "Lock up the food? What the hell is wrong with you—can't you control yourself?"

"Can't you control *your*self?" I would scream back at him, even though I was scared shitless. My dad—short, stocky, pudgy—had his own issues with weight and food, and maybe that's why he took it out on me—something about me reminded him of what he despised in himself. When he ate, he attacked the food, the world around him disappeared, and nothing else mattered except shoveling in that next bite, and the next and the next and the next. He would literally stuff his face, eating so fast, and taking such huge mouthfuls, he'd stop breathing, nearly choke, and his face would turn bright red. It was really difficult to watch.

* * *

Undaunted, and more determined than ever to get as skinny as my dad wanted me to be, I made my third trip to Camp Napanoch in the summer of 1970, when I was 13. One day I was walking back to my bunk when I was nearly kidnapped for the second time. Our cabins were large and dormitory-style. You would walk up the stairs in the middle of the building and then go either right or left to the bedrooms on either side. At the end of each hallway was a door that opened to stairs that led outside and down to ground level. On this particular day, I was going back to my room after lunch (or at least what passed for "lunch" at fat camp; cordon bleu cooking, it was not). I walked up the central staircase and at the top, I turned right to head to my room. But then I saw a man standing at the end of the hallway near the door. He immediately looked out of place at a summer camp, his hair clipped and neatly combed, and dressed formally, wearing a dark suit with dark jacket and tie, just like one of the men who had approached me in the limo. He was staring at me with such focus and energy that I just knew, instinctively, that he had come for me. I started to scream bloody murder, at the top of my lungs.

And then I must have blacked out, because the next thing I knew, the man was gone. People came and someone gently led me outside and sat with me in the grass, stroking my hand and talking softly as I tried to catch my breath. I was in shock. How could this happen? *Even at camp I'm not safe? If the mob can get to me here, then they can get to me anywhere. None of us are safe.* But I also started to do some quick figuring. I had now survived two kidnapping attempts, and Jarrett had survived one. I couldn't help but wonder—*Is there something special about the Hodas children that makes us kidnap-proof?*

They searched the campgrounds but the man was gone—there was no sign of him anywhere. Amazingly, the only thing I could think about was whether I should tell Mom or not. I still remembered how upset she'd been when Jarrett was taken, and I didn't want to push her over the edge again. But of course, I didn't have a choice. The camp administrators had to tell my parents. Even after my parents were informed of this terrifying incident, they didn't come to get me and whisk me back home, and they never offered any kind words, support, or reassurance. I remained at camp for the rest of the summer as if nothing had happened, totally vulnerable and without any protection.

Which, as it turned out, wasn't all bad, in the end. Because that summer, I met Knuckles. I met Knuckles and, thanks to him, I discovered foreplay. And once I discovered foreplay, life, as I knew it, would never be the same again.

Chapter Seven

First Love and Wicked Knuckleballs
1970

You might think that as the Princess of 42nd Street, the daughter of Times Square's King of Porn, Lord of the Loops, and Merchant of Sleaze, my whole life would have been suffused with sex, right from day one. You might imagine that sex toys littered my bedroom floor and I learned the facts of life from discarded copies of *Playboy* and *Hustler*. And it is true that once I was 14 or 15, porn became a large part of my life as I started hanging out at Dad's adult bookstores and met some of the girls who worked for him, getting to know them and learning what led them to a life selling their bodies.

But all that came later, well into adolescence. My early years were surprisingly wholesome and innocent, sexually speaking, especially before I really knew and understood what my father did for a living, back when I still saw him as the guy who busted sacks of quarters out of cigarette and vending machines and brought them home like pirate's booty, pouring them out like a slick, silver river across our kitchen table.

I do want to emphasize here that, even though our dad's business was porn and the exploitation, marketing and selling of women's bodies, he was never sexual with us, his children. He never touched us inappropriately, never asked us to be in his films when we were older. He was a terrible father in many ways, but incest wasn't one of his hobbies.

My own sexual awakening came in the summer of 1970, when I turned 13 and went to fat camp for the third time. Camp had just started and we were having a barbeque. I was at the end of the line and started talking to a guy I hadn't met before. I noticed right away that he was cute—imagine a young Fonzie from *Happy Days* and you get the picture. This boy was a little shorter than me and not so fat—in fact, to me, he didn't seem overweight at all, from what I could see. *What the fuck were our parents doing to us?!* Anyway, this guy had thick, wavy brown hair, brown eyes, and wore glasses. And boy, did he have an attitude! Twelve years old and totally sure of himself. I liked him right away—his swagger, his style, his confidence. He was someone I wanted to know better

"Hi, I'm Knuckles," he said, extending his hand as we inched forward in the line.

"Knuckles? Your name is Knuckles?!" I asked. "What the hell kind of name is that?"

If he was insulted, he didn't show it. "They call me Knuckles because I throw a wicked knuckleball," he explained, demonstrating the grip with his fingertips and thumb. "When I'm on, no one can touch my stuff." His real name was Barry Stein, and we soon became the hot couple at camp. For the first time in my life, I was in love.

The previous year at camp I had met a beautiful little brown-haired girl from Pennsylvania named Caren, and we'd both come back this summer and resumed our friendship, but as soon as I met Knuckles, I left Caren to find other friends as I spent all my time with him. I did feel bad about it, but young love is a speeding freight train you just can't derail—you gotta follow that locomotive all the way to the end of the line. And, boy, this was the beginning of more fun than I had ever known. I wanted to be with Knuckles anytime I could.

We spent much of that summer sitting in the wooden gazebo with his head in my lap and me stroking his hair, running my fingers through those thick, dark waves, listening to crickets and cicadas and letting the warm breeze fan our skin. What a feeling! This was a bliss I had never felt before. Knuckles was just so cool, even the older girls at camp had crushes on him, but I knew he was crazy about me.

It was all so wonderfully new and fresh and innocent as we began to explore love—and each other. One afternoon, we sneaked away from swimming or first aid or lanyard-braiding, whatever it was they had us doing to pass the time, and met someplace we knew we'd have privacy—the edge of a long wooden bridge that arched over the river and connected to a field that led directly to The Shanty, a bar/nightclub in the distance, closer to town.

Knuckles and I met at the bridge and started making out. In a

The Princess of 42nd Street

matter of moments, I was lost in kissing him. He was the first boy I had ever kissed like this, and it made my heart dance and my body feel exciting new things. We were making out like crazy when suddenly I felt Knuckles touch my breast, over my shirt. I could not believe it. What was this feeling? As he caressed my nipple, I went into another world. I could not believe how good it felt.

Suddenly, though, I jumped up, pulling away from him. *Oh my God—what have I done? Did I just let a boy feel me up?* I started running and I ran, crying, all the way back to the dorm where I collapsed, sobbing, in my bunk. *I think I just did something bad. Aren't only adults supposed to do things like that?* I wondered. Caren and two other girls I was close to came in to talk to me.

"What the hell happened?" Caren asked, breathless as she sat beside me. She lifted my arm and tried to see if I was hurt. "Are you okay? Romola, what happened?"

How do I tell them this terrible thing I did? What will they think of me if they know? Will they think I'm slutty or whorish?

"C'mon, Romola, you gotta tell us so we can help you," my friend Nina said.

I could hold it in no longer. "I-I-I let Knuckles feel me up!" I choked out, then dissolved again into sobs, burying my face in the damp pillow. The girls talked to me very gently and tried to reassure me, calming me down. Strangely, during this time, the girls would go out of the room one at a time and then come back in. When I asked Caren about it months later, she said they were taking turns to go outside and laugh where I couldn't hear them. Wow, not like that's embarrassing or anything.

Anyway, I soon made amends with Knuckles, told him I was okay, and we continued seeing each other. We became inseparable, and anytime we could be together, we were. But I never let him touch me again… until one night.

To explain, I need to backtrack a bit. There was a girl at camp named Robin who had a crush on Knuckles. She was about three years older than him, but there was something about him that even the older girls were drawn to. Well, I found out that he and Robin had been seeing each other behind my back. I was heartbroken and hysterical, and immediately told him I could not see him anymore. I saw the hurt in his eyes, but at that moment, I didn't care.

It seemed like the whole camp knew something was up. I remember sitting on the grass, crying my eyes out. Then word came that Knuckles wanted to talk to me. I was hesitant but agreed to see him. He apologized profusely, explaining that he needed something that I couldn't give him. He begged me to take him back. And I did, because I kind of understood what he meant. And I was really crazy about him.

That summer, Knuckles and I were chosen as the King and Queen of Camp Napanoch. I even got to dress up and be paraded around in some kind of cart. I couldn't believe it—me, the deformed little fat girl, Fat Moley, the imbecile, was suddenly Queen of the Camp. I wished the summer would last forever and I would never have to go home.

The adventures continued. One day I was in the gazebo with Knuckles and two friends, Earl and Ken. Earl was a short, chubby, brown-haired kid from Brooklyn. Ken was older, taller, and had brown hair and glasses. Like so many of the campers, he did not appear to be overweight at all.

While at the gazebo, the guys revealed that they were planning a raid of The Shanty! Now, if I remember correctly, these masterminds had already gone into the kitchen one night and stolen some ice cream. (In the interest of full disclosure, my first two years at camp, I lost 12 to 15 pounds. This third year, perhaps not surprisingly, I lost a grand total of six.

Anyway, back to the "big heist." The guys were planning to sneak over the wooden bridge where Knuckles had felt me up and through the field to The Shanty in the distance... at 12:00 midnight. And they wanted me to join them; to play "Bonnie" to their collection of "Clydes," in other words.

"No way; I am not going with you," I protested. "It's way too dangerous. They'll call our parents and send us home if we get caught!"

"C'mon, it will be fun," Knuckles promised. So, I went with them, and it was amazing. I sneaked out of my bunk in the middle of the night as we had agreed and met the ringleaders at the edge of the wooden bridge. The night was clear and the moon so bright that we could see everything around us.

The bridge swung back and forth as we tiptoed over it, me and Knuckles and Ken and Earl, along with another friend, Wayne; my sister Risa; and a couple of other guys as well. Risa still recalls this as one of the best nights of her life—she said she felt like she was in a movie.

Once we were over the bridge, we took off running through the field, Knuckles holding my hand as we ran, our feet slicing through the thick grass, pounding the firm-packed earth beneath. When we reached The Shanty, we cleared the shelves, stuffing our pockets with sweet, sugary booty—O. Henry bars, Snickers, Baby Ruths, Almond Joy, $100,000 Bars, taking everything in sight. If the staff of The Shanty had any suspicions about underage fat camp refugees clearing out their candy stock in the middle of the night, they kept those suspicions to themselves.

Now, bringing our spoils back to camp was like taking a pitcher of martinis to an AA meeting. I don't remember if, besides eating a lot of the candy ourselves, we sold the candy to the kids back at camp or if, feeling more benevolent, we gave it away. But I certainly remember what came next that night.

Knuckles and I ran, hand in hand, all the way back to his cabin. His bunk was the one on top. There was a window there and it was open, allowing in a light, beautiful breeze. After knowing what went on between him and Robin, how much further they had gone than we had, and being so curious and wanting to feel that incredible feeling again, I lay back and let him lift up my shirt, placing his mouth on my breast. All thoughts disappeared and I was filled with magical sensations. I started to moan with pleasure, making so much noise, Knuckles had to stop and shush me.

"No, I will be quiet, please don't stop," I begged him, running my fingers through his thick hair and pulling his head back to my nipple.

Heaven. It was absolute heaven. I just knew that if I was doing this with someone I liked and felt deeply about, it couldn't be wrong. I wanted to go further, but I didn't let him do anything more. It didn't occur to me to touch him or explore his body; that thought never even crossed my mind. And slipping his hand between my legs? No, never considered it, and I don't think he even tried. Boy, he was an angel, an unlikely angel with glasses and a wicked knuckleball.

As the days of camp wound down, and the shorter, cooler nights let me know that the summer was slipping away, I dreaded going home. No boys at home were interested in me; I didn't think any boys ever would be. I would go back to being the fat, ugly loser I imagined myself to be. Of course, if I had really known what awaited me back in Lawrence, I probably would have run away and hidden out in the Catskills forever, found a shack in the woods and just holed up there, because soon, my entire life, and the lives of my whole family, would be turned upside down, changed forever.

Chapter Eight

Sex Parties, Porn Stars and Swimming Pools
1970-1971

After that blissful summer of 1970 spent at fat camp, where I lost a miniscule amount of weight (six measly pounds) but gained my first great love (Barry "Knuckles" Stein), I returned home to our mini-mansion in Lawrence, two months into my teenage years and ready to start eighth grade at Lawrence Junior High with a smile on my face, a spring in my step and a new lease on life.

And... yeah. That lasted all of about 15 minutes. Things had been really good between my parents when we first moved to Lawrence in 1968, but now, only two years later, things were deteriorating rapidly. Dad was heavily into drink and drugs as he faced increasing pressure from the police, the DA, the mob, and other forces, and Mom was sliding back into the depths of her mental illness, retreating from us and from the world, into a dark, silent, hopeless place where she was as cold and hard as stone and where no one could reach her.

It got so bad that eighth-grade autumn that I would do anything I could *not* to have to go home after school. Hang out with friends, go shopping at Cedarhurst (Five Towns' version of Fifth Avenue), hell, I would have volunteered to bang erasers, mop the floors, and wash the chalkboards if it would have given me precious moments away from the hell that awaited me at 37 Harborview West. But I knew my siblings needed me, and I felt guilty leaving them alone, at the mercy of our parents, so inevitably I would trudge my way back along broad, unbroken Lawrence Avenue to that big house on the water, my heart cascading to my feet the moment I walked through the front door.

Usually, the first person I saw when I got home was Carolina, just one of a number in our ongoing series of live-in maids, many of whom only lasted a few weeks or months, unwilling or unable to put up with the constant yelling, screaming and chaos that defined the Hodas home. Invariably, Carolina had a bottle of Pepsi squeezed between her arm and her enormous torso and was chewing a massive wad of gum. Seriously, she must have put five or six pieces in there at once and started chewing away. The only thing she could cook was fried chicken, so, needless to say, we ate *a lot* of fried chicken in those days.

Mom would be sequestered upstairs in her room, just sitting in the dark, crying, staring into space, listening to John Denver records. None of us at the time realized how terribly ill she was; we just thought she was sad and very angry, and that was the saddest part of my life, having her physically so close by, and yet with no way to reach her, to pierce her dark shell of despair.

As the clock inched closer to 6:00 p.m., I would start rounding up the kids, telling them, "Get into your rooms! Hurry! Daddy'll be home any minute!" I knew he would be in a foul, frightening mood when he arrived home from work, coming down hard and fast from an intense high fueled by cocaine or Black Beauty amphetamines, and until he leveled off with a couple of glasses of vodka on ice, he'd be violent and unpredictable, dangerous as a freshly sharpened blade.

I'm upstairs in my bedroom when I hear him burst through the front door and stomp to the kitchen, going to the refrigerator and pulling on the door so hard, he nearly tips the fridge. "What the hell is this?" he screams. "This fucking pear is rotten! You people waste all MY money!" *Smash!* He throws the pear back into the refrigerator and guzzles down some milk.

Now he's on his way upstairs, feet pounding each step, looking for trouble, ready to raise hell with anyone bold enough, or stupid enough, to get in his way. He stomps down the hall to my bedroom and with one quick, decisive motion, throws open my bedroom door, looks me dead in the eye and stares me down, silently, looking for a reason to berate me. Inside, I'm quaking, but I stand firm, holding strong, daring and defying him, silently taunting, *C'mon, I dare you, old man, lay a finger on me or one of those kids and you* will *be sorry.*

The Princess of 42nd Street

He closes my door, stomps to the room shared by Risa and Rhonda, and flings open their door so hard it hits the wall and bounces back. "What's all this shit on the floor? I want you to CLEAN IT UP NOW!" he bellows, and I can just picture Risa and Rhonda, 11 and nine, cowering at the corners of their beds, terrified. I have to do something—now. I open my bedroom door and step into the hallway.

"Dad, why don't you go downstairs, make yourself a drink, and eat some chicken?" I say evenly, not raising my voice. "Carolina made it fresh. Let us do our homework." He wheels on me and with one swift move, the back of his hand raises, ready to smash my face. "Who do you think you are, talking to me like that?" he yells.

I step back, look at him, and shake my head. "You fat, fucking bastard," I whisper under my breath so he can't hear, and then say louder, "Please, Dad, stay away from them—leave us alone!"

And he whirls back again, walks about ten steps to the master bedroom, and starts in on Mom, badgering and berating her, humiliating her and calling her names. "The house is a fucking mess, Paula! Why the hell can't you get the housekeeper to clean? What the fuck do we pay her for?" he screams.

I breathe a huge sigh of relief. Tonight, he backed down, but that doesn't always happen. For example, there was one Sunday morning when I was 14 and we were all in the kitchen eating the bagels and lox Dad had brought home after his weekly game of handball. He was feeling hard and flushed and happy, convinced he'd just sweated out a week's worth of drugs and drink and other damage. Risa, age 12, accidently spilled some milk on the table—what a cliché, spilled milk—but Dad exploded. He grabbed Risa's hand and slammed it hard on the table, and just as he was about to hit her, I jumped up from my seat and lunged at him.

"Don't you dare touch her!" I yelled, trying to get between them. He balled up his fist and punched me so hard in the back I fell to the ground. And suddenly, I couldn't get up. *I can't move! Oh my God—I'm paralyzed!* I was too shocked and terrified to cry. *What's wrong with me? Why can't I move my arms or legs? What has he done to me?*

Mom must have been in her studio that day because, unbelievably, she heard the commotion and came downstairs. Once she saw the state I was in, she helped me get up as the feeling gradually returned to my limbs. I must have been in really bad shape because Mom drove me straight to the ER to get checked out. When the doctors asked me what happened, how I got hurt, I said, "My dad hit me. He punched me in the back." And that was that—no social services, no investigation, no calls to CPS. Back in the '70s, if your dad hit you, that was just tough luck for you, I suppose.

I was diagnosed with muscle spasms and given some drugs for muscle relaxation and pain relief. When we got home, Dad never asked how I was, never checked to see if I was okay. I didn't talk to him for a few days, but after that, things returned to normal. Or at least what passed for normal in the Hodas house of horrors.

The one bright spot during these dark times was Knuckles, and through Knuckles, there was Earl, and through Earl, there was Joey, the gorgeous, enticing boy who would become my first husband. Knuckles only lived half an hour away from me, in North Massapequa Park, Long Island.

I missed him so much once we got home from camp, and I was so excited when he called me that fall and invited me over to his house. I had visions of continuing our summer romance, but then he took me downstairs to his basement and we started to get intimate. Which was fine, until he grabbed my hand and shoved it down his pants. I was shocked to feel this hot, hard thing down there, covered with so much hair. I was so grossed out, I broke up with him the next day. I still wasn't ready for where he wanted to take our relationship.

Even after breaking up with Knuckles, I kept in touch by phone with our friend Earl from camp. On March 25, 1971, a day that will live in my memory forever, Earl invited me to come visit him in Brooklyn and hang out with his friends Joey, Cary and Brian. And suddenly, there he was, this boy named Joey, in full 1970s' poster-boy glory, age 15 to my 13, with his tall frame, narrow hips and muscular arms, and his wavy brown hair that was parted in the middle and fell to his shoulders. His background was Italian and Irish, with a broad smile and high cheekbones.

The moment I met Joey, my feelings for Knuckles started to fade away. As we all hung out in Joey's basement that day, listening to music, smoking pot and talking on his waterbed, I felt a seismic shift in my life—something significant had changed forever. I would soon know love, real love, physical love, in a way I never had before.

The Princess of 42nd Street

* * *

Meanwhile, back at the Hodas homestead, there were drugs, and there was drinking. But even with the drugs and the drinking, there were still appetites to be sated, desires to be indulged, fantasies to be fulfilled. And that's when my parents' swinging and sex orgies began. It's really pretty remarkable that I have any normal, healthy ideas about sex whatsoever, considering the depravity I witnessed in my own Long Island living room during those crazy days in the early '70s, when I was still only in my mid-teens.

Apparently, Dad didn't get enough sexual stimulation running a porn empire at work, so he started hosting swinger parties at home—basically, parties where people arrived as a couple and then switched partners to have sex, and then switched again, until everyone had enjoyed multiple partners in one night. From what I remember, the party attendees were generally eight couples, friends of Mom and Dad's from Goldie's, the good-looking, nouveau riche who liked Dad, and who especially liked the cheap, easy sex and drugs he made available to them.

We kids were supposed to stay upstairs in our rooms during these parties, but of course we were curious and wanted to explore. As the oldest, I thought it okay for me to look and then prevent my sisters and brother from seeing anything they shouldn't, but they disagreed. This caused a lot of arguing among me and my siblings because they wanted to see what was going on too, while I was doing all I could to prevent that from happening.

I did the best I could, but still, they were exposed to far too much. For example, Jarrett told me just recently that he remembers being a kid and seeing Dad outside floating naked on an inner tube in the swimming pool and sporting a full erection. It still breaks my heart to think about all the things those kids had to try to make sense of at such a young age.

Often during these parties, I found myself tiptoeing to the top of the staircase or peering around dark corners, watching people get drunk, get high and have sex. I watched people chop up lines of coke on the kitchen counter and snort it up their nose, then run naked and screaming down the hallway, licking cocaine residue from their fingers. Men sacked out spread-eagle on the sofa with their pants circling their ankles, naked women kneeling in front of them, giving blow jobs. People were having sex everywhere—the kitchen, the bathrooms, the living room, the basement, out by the pool. Once, I even caught a couple having sex in Jarrett's bed. Fortunately, Jarrett wasn't there at the time.

The doorbell would ring repeatedly, all night long, and people would enter, shouting, "Kingy! Hey, Kingy! Get me a drink!" and my flesh would crawl, having to listen to it. "Kingy" was Dad's nickname, as he was steadily building his reputation as Times Square's undisputed "King of Porn." All I could think about was protecting my younger siblings. I was only 14, so they were 12, ten, and eight—precious young children who never should have been exposed to these adult things.

Perhaps inevitably, the lines between the adult world and our world blurred. One time, Risa, her friend, Joyce, and I found a tray of brownies on the counter in the kitchen. We assumed someone had dropped them off for the swingers' party that night. They looked delicious, so we dug in and devoured some of them, shoving the rich, gooey chocolate goodness into our mouths.

And then afterward, I knew right away what was wrong, why I felt so sluggish and giggly and just wanted to lie in bed and listen to my records—the brownies had been laced with pot. But Risa and Joyce were only 12 and had never gotten high before, so the pot made them feel weird and scared. I didn't want to tell them they were getting high because I didn't want to scare them more than they already were. It took a while for the pot to leave our systems, and I was furious at my parents for exposing us to drugs. This time it was only pot, but what if next time it was coke or speed or heroin?

Another time, the swingers' party had gone on until the early morning hours. Unable to sleep with all the noise and chaos, I crept out of my bedroom and stood at the top of the stairs, peering through the railing to the lower level. There I saw a woman who I knew worked as a topless waitress, clutching a little fuzzy black kitten to her naked chest and breastfeeding it as if it were her baby, walking around and showing everyone what she was doing.

A kitten? What the hell? What is wrong with these people? What is wrong with my parents? How gross, disgusting and perverted it all seemed. I turned around and there was Risa behind me, shocked, staring at the unbelievable scene. I tried to shield her eyes, but it was too late—she had already seen too much.

I want out, I told myself. *I want out of here. I can't live like this anymore. But I can't leave the kids. I have to find a way to help us all. Why does Mom let Dad do this?* I felt she should have stepped in to stop it, to protect her own children, but she had so many demons of her own, maybe she felt it was easier just to go along with it. All she had to do was let us sleep at friends' houses—I didn't get it. A part of me came to hate both Mom and Dad for what they were doing to us. I hated that this was destroying Risa, Rhonda and Jarrett's innocence at such young ages.

Another time, I was outside watching as two couples swam over to the shallow end of the pool, stripped off their bathing suits, and started having sex in the water. These four people would later go on to become famous porn stars, but at the time, I only knew them as people who hung out at my parents' parties. Mom was there too, watching everything, but she just stood there like a statue, mute, not moving a muscle.

I headed toward the couples intending to say, "Get the fuck out of the pool, this is my mother's home and she doesn't want you here," but one of my parents' friends whom I liked a great deal, Mrs. Leibowitz, stepped into my path and stopped me, urging, "Romola, go inside now. You shouldn't be seeing this. You know your father. He likes to shock people."

"Mrs. Leibowitz," I said defiantly, holding my ground. "This is my mother's home, too. Look at her; she doesn't want this. Can't you see how unhappy she is?"

Mrs. Leibowitz shook her head sadly. "Go upstairs, Romola," she said softly. "You shouldn't be here."

I went inside, climbed the stairs, and sat down on the top step, wrapping my arms around my knees and pulling them toward my chest. I watched the sick, sordid tableau of sex and drugs playing itself out in our living room beneath me. *Why am I here, at this "pool party," with these leeches and losers and hangers-on?* I asked myself. *What is wrong with us? What's wrong with our world?* I was only 14 and yet I felt worry and despair far beyond my years.

I've lost my dad forever, I realized. *That Daddy I had until I was eight, the Daddy I would wait for when I was three or four years old, sitting on the curb in Bethpage anxious for him to round the corner in his station wagon so I could run to meet him in the driveway, and laugh with glee as he threw me high in the air again and again, catching me every time in his strong, safe, gentle arms. That was the Daddy who loved me, who protected me from Mom,* I thought, *and now he's gone forever. I'll never see* that *Daddy again.*

Chapter Nine

Hanging Out with Strippers, Vacationing with the Mob
1971

By the time I was 14, I think I had pretty much figured out what my father did for a living, even if most of the sordid, salacious details were still a bit hazy. I knew his job wasn't like other dads', I knew he wasn't a doctor or a lawyer or a bricklayer, he didn't carry a union membership card, punch a time clock, and trudge home from the bus stop every evening at 5:00 p.m. with his hard hat and lunchbox in tow.

And while I knew he was engaged in a business that wasn't like other dads', the precise nature of his employment wasn't exactly fodder for dinner table conversation.

"How was work today, Dad?"

"It was fine, honey. I hired three strippers, ordered ten cases of dildos, two boxes of Ben Wa balls, produced ten new porn films, and renewed the lease on a couple of massage parlors. How'd you do on your geometry quiz?"

I not only sensed what my father did for a living, I was also becoming aware that he hung around with some very shady characters, guys who were more than just small-time hoods, or from the wrong side of the tracks. I knew that every morning before work, Dad would come downstairs, open the large wooden cabinet in the kitchen, take out his handgun, stick it in his inside jacket pocket, and leave to catch the 8:20 train into Manhattan. Clearly, there was someone, or something, that made him feel he needed protection.

And there were other signs as well. For example, the summer I was 12, the whole family vacationed in the Catskills, staying at the Concord Resort Hotel with Dad's friend and associate Joseph Brocchini and Joe's wife and kids. They seemed nice enough; didn't make much of an impression on me, to be honest. But it turns out, this same Joseph Brocchini, aka "Joe Bikini," was a notorious "made man" in the Lucchese crime family and would be murdered, execution-style, seven years later, in 1976, when someone shot him five times in the back of the head and left his body in the office of the used car dealership he owned. Coincidentally (or maybe not so coincidentally), Joe Bikini had been scheduled to meet with my dad later that same morning to discuss a business deal.

Clearly, Martin Hodas moved in some dangerous circles. And yet... we had a kind of collective "reality blindness" going on at home. Dad swore to us, up and down, that he had no association with the mob whatsoever. And we chose to believe him. Maybe it was just easier that way. One time I came home from school and Dad was there with all these rough-looking guys sitting around the kitchen table, having some kind of porn-related pow-wow. Dad stopped mid-sentence when I walked in and said sharply, "Hey, Louie, stop checking out my daughter's tits!" Far from being embarrassed or intimidated, I found this hilarious, because after Dad said that, the guys all became very well-mannered and a little shy around me, even deferential.

At the same time, I was so worried about Mom. As she descended deeper and deeper into mental illness, she started taking to her bed for longer and longer periods, eventually up to six months at a time. At the time, we didn't know that Mom was bipolar (the condition was not as well understood then as it is today). I thought that it was because of how Dad treated her that she stayed in bed all day. I thought he was jealous of her, so he controlled and undermined her, knowing that his constant berating of her would destroy her confidence and keep her bedbound. And perhaps that was a part of it, but clearly, there was a lot more going on.

Her behavior was so hard for me to understand. Sometimes she would be up in the mornings, screaming at me, and then when I came home from school in the afternoon, she would be kind and loving, behaving just like a normal mom, asking me about my day. I would look at her and say, "You cannot be serious—the way you treated me this morning, and now, all of a sudden you're June Cleaver? You must be kidding me. School was horrible." Even when it seemed like she was reaching out to me, I rarely let my guard down, because I knew that in a few hours, she could turn vicious again. What a sad, hopeless mess it all was.

This would go on for the better part of ten years, on and off, with

The Princess of 42nd Street

these long, deep, endless depressions where she was heavily drugged, interspersed with brief, manic "highs," when she would draw, paint and sculpt. At one point, she would even go back to school and fall in love with her art teacher, Mishu. I begged her, "Mom, please leave Dad. Leave him and go with Mishu—he can make you happy." I don't know if Mishu even knew how Mom felt about him, or if anything substantial ever happened between them.

Despite Mom's occasional highs, inevitably, the downward spiral would begin again. It was soul-crushing and exhausting as I increasingly had to take over as "parent in charge," making sure that the kids were provided for in whatever way I could.

I knew we couldn't go on like this, as a family, without falling apart completely. I also knew the family I came from. Instinctively, even at that young age, I knew that if I didn't learn how to talk kindlier and be more compassionate and positive to myself, I would be screwed for life. I asked Mom to get me, to get all of us, into therapy. And I must have been a good salesperson even at that young age, because after much begging from me, Mom found a therapist. Dad, as you can probably imagine, was less than thrilled, and he refused to let Jarrett go.

"You know psychiatrists have the highest rate of suicide of any profession!" he would scream. I didn't know if that was true, but I did know that I needed a teacher, a mentor, somebody to help me, my siblings, and my difficult and strange mother. I knew I would be Romola Hodas just this once, and I was going to find out how to be good to her and figure out what made her happy. It is so much easier to be unhappy. We have to learn what makes us happy and then apply what we've learned to our lives. I believed that then just as I believe it now.

Even though Mom agreed to get us into therapy, it was hardly smooth sailing. After the very first session with the first therapist, the guy announced to Mom that, having spoken to me for all of 30 minutes, he could say with absolute certainty that I was doomed to either become a lesbian or commit suicide. *Great! Happy news! And this is supposed to help me* how, *exactly?*

I assured Mom that I'd never be gay, I certainly didn't feel suicidal, and we needed to find another therapist. Eventually we found dear old Dr. Henry Schwartz. Dr. Schwartz was a hypnotist, and he would have me lie down on the white sofa in his office and relax as he "hypnotized" me. While I was supposedly "under," he would tell me how much I hated myself and how I needed to take action and make some changes in my life! What the hell was he thinking, saying this to a vulnerable teenage girl? And more to the point, why did Mom allow this? Maybe Dr. Schwartz had found a way to manipulate her. Or maybe she was just lonely, and happy to have someone to talk to other than Dad, who constantly demeaned and abused her.

We ended up seeing Dr. Schwartz for a long time, probably five or six years. He lived near us in Lawrence, in a big, beautiful house that I imagine we helped pay for. It was so strange and upsetting when he suddenly, out of the blue, just stopped seeing me and refused to give me any more appointments. I had really grown to depend on him after all this time, so I kept calling him to get an explanation and find out what was wrong. After I left a number of long messages, he finally, reluctantly, agreed to see me one final time.

"Why did you just stop seeing me?" I asked over and over as I confronted him in his office, demanding an explanation. I can still picture him getting up and standing behind his chair, grasping the back with his hands and squeezing until his knuckles turned white. He was a slim, short man with thinning blond hair.

"I realized I have been treating you the wrong way; my work with you has not been correct," he explained, not making eye contact.

I was so shocked, it took me a moment to find my voice. "Not been *correct*?" I asked. "What are you saying? You realized you have been treating us wrong, so you just stop seeing us?"

He nodded.

"So are you telling me that if you saw that you were bringing up your own daughters in a way that was wrong and realized that you needed to parent differently, you would just shove them off to private school or throw them away? Wouldn't you instead start to rear them in the new way you decided was best?" I argued. He just shrugged.

So he was saying he realized that for five or six years, he really had no business working with my whole family, and when he realized this, he just stopped taking my calls and making appointments. I am assuming he did the same thing to the rest of my family. I was crushed and felt so alone and abandoned.

The Princess of 42nd Street

"No, Dr. Schwartz, this is not acceptable," I said, refusing to accept his non-response. "After the kids and I and my mom are so invested in you, you can't just drop us, just leave us like this. You need to be responsible and fix what you destroyed." But in the end, he did nothing. It took a long time for me to forgive him. I do believe, though, that I gained something positive from our sessions. I have always sought out a counselor when I felt life was too hard to handle on my own.

I'm still not sure how much damage was done to us by Dr. Schwartz. He made a pretty penny on the Hodas family, that's for sure. For me, this was just another in a series of deep disappointments. I wanted so badly to help myself, my mother and my younger siblings, but even the people whose job it was to help us, people like Dr. Schwartz, seemed to care more about themselves than about us, and I found myself alone yet again, shipwrecked in my own personal sea of pain and fear.

* * *

As my family's wealth grew, so did my curiosity about my dad's business. *What goes on at Dad's bookstores, photo studios and other establishments?* I wondered. *What are all these people paying so much money to see and do?*

Eventually I got up the courage to ask Mom, during one of her rare lucid moments, why Dad owned these sex shops. Why did he hire women to take off their clothes and perform nude for strangers, on film and in real life?

Her response was remarkably matter-of-fact. "Romola, it's a way to provide a legal and honest service to people who need this kind of thing," she explained. "And the girls make good money, so it helps them, too."

I knew the money was good, but money alone didn't make it a safe or respectable career and lifestyle.

"But Romola, that's why we're so rich," Mom emphasized. "Because all sorts of people like sex. Some men's wives or girlfriends won't do certain things that they like, so they go to Dad's stores to watch girls, or they watch Triple-X movies. Your father is not involved in animal or child porn. These are consenting men and women."

When Mom talked about Dad's porn business, she made it sound reasonable, rational, even desirable. And yet I knew things were not as simple and straightforward as they seemed on the surface. There was a reason people talked about porn in hushed tones, if they talked about it at all, and why the topic of adult entertainment didn't come up in polite conversation.

At some point, I decided I needed to find out for myself what this mysterious world was all about. I had visited Dad's office, but I had never been to one of his stores, and I felt like I needed to know what went on there. I got up the courage to go upstairs at one of Dad's porn shops and introduced myself to the women who performed the live sex shows. They were so surprised to see "Marty's daughter" show up to talk to them and ask them about their lives.

It took me some time to earn their trust, but once I did, they started to open up to me. We talked in their dressing room, the air thick and damp with a sour combination of sweat, cigarette smoke, perfume and Aqua Net. Dressed in flimsy robes (or less) and stiletto heels, they chewed gum and gossiped as they slapped on their cheap, garish makeup; curled and sprayed their hair into high towers atop their heads, bummed cigarettes off each other and laughed at their own little in-jokes.

Slowly, carefully, I drew out their stories. I think I may have been one of the few people to really care about who they were, as women, not as objects, which was why they felt comfortable confiding in me. Some of their stories were disturbing, some were funny, many were heartbreaking. I listened without judgment and just let them talk.

The girls told me about posing for photos for porn magazines, and how they had to mimic sex positions like the "standing bridesmaid." Apparently, this involved the model turning her back to the camera and thrusting out her butt cheek. One girl demonstrated for me, then burst out giggling. Other positions included the cowgirl, the sidesaddle, the dirty doggie, the scissor, the 69, the reverse blow job, the wheelbarrow, and the American split, among others. Well, I was certainly gaining an education!! I could describe for you all the details of these sexual gymnastics, but instead, I'm just going to say that the human body is amazingly *flexible,* and you can Google the rest.

We laughed about some of photoshoots, but then the conversation turned darker. Heroin addiction. STDs. Abortion. Domestic violence. Childhood sexual abuse. Girls who ran away at 14 because life on the street was safer and less scary than life at home. One girl at age 20 was already divorced and stripping to support her two kids. Another was hoping to raise money to put herself through cosmetology school.

Drugs, especially coke and amphetamines, were ubiquitous, and the girls downed pills like handfuls of candy. Black Beauties (also known as Black Birds or Black Bombers) were a favorite. Girls needed drugs to ramp themselves up for the shows, then needed downers, Quaaludes and alcohol, to come down afterward, and perhaps to help them forget the things they'd seen and done.

I learned about the different levels of porn. Some girls only posed for photos; some posed and stripped, some posed, stripped *and* performed in films and on stage. But the girls who actually let the men touch them made the most money of all. Some earned more than $500 a day, and this was the early '70s, when a loaf of bread cost 25 cents and gas was 50 cents a gallon, so $500 was a fortune, and these girls could earn that in a single day.

Blondie's story, in particular, has always stuck with me. She worked in the back room giving private peep shows and was bone-thin, had stringy, bleached-blonde hair and haunting blue eyes. She also had a heavy cocaine habit, two ex-husbands, and a little boy she rarely saw. Her boyfriend beat her; her parents disowned her. Her plan was to just do porn until she'd saved up enough to leave the city and move upstate with her son, where they'd live in the country and raise rabbits and chickens. When I saw her at the porn shop several years later, she was still doing the peep shows. Her son was in foster care, her eyes were vacant and she looked decades older than her actual age of 27.

After I'd met and befriended some of the Dad's "girls," I explored the stores a bit more. I told myself I was doing research as I went in and introduced myself as "Marty's daughter." Once the managers and staff knew who I was, they gave me a wide berth, and this is where I *really* got an education.

VHS recorders hadn't hit the market yet, so the explosion in renting or buying porn tapes was still in the future, but the stores sold

8 mm and Super-8 porn films that could be shown on a projector at home. Aisle after aisle of the store was filled with pornographic books while porn magazines were arranged in tall stacks on the floor. These mags ranged from the almost-mainstream *Hustler*, *Penthouse*, *Playboy* and *SCREW*, to much more hardcore periodicals such as *Climax*, *Intercum*, *Cunt Hunter*, *Tits for Two* and *Pussyrama*. The covers of these periodicals were pretty explicit; I can only imagine what was inside!

The walls of the store featured row after row of dildos, vibrators, handcuffs, dental dams, butt plugs and all kinds of S&M gear including whips, chains, leashes, leather gear and black masks with zippers that closed over the eyes and mouth. Also, Ben Wa Balls, aka "Orgasm Balls," marble-sized balls, hollow and containing a small weight that rolled around inside the ball. These balls were inserted in the vagina by the user to increase sexual stimulation.

What the hell do people do with all these things in their bedrooms, anyway? I wondered. Suddenly, Joey and I didn't seem very adventurous.

I also explored the infamous "peep show" booths that had made Dad so much money, and then the "live" peep show booths. Here a guy would go into a booth, put in his quarter, and then look through the slot to see six or seven naked girls dancing, gyrating and touching themselves as they twirled around a rotating stage. The slots were big enough for a guy to stick his hand through so he could touch the girls, and maybe, if he was adventurous, he could stick his finger in one girl's vagina, or if he were limber enough, stick his penis in to get a blow job.

One of the managers, a guy named Mike, was especially good in letting me hang out in the store during business hours, and I'd watch as sometimes a guy would come in and after talking to Mike for a while, Mike would reach under the counter and pull out something, maybe something more hardcore, and sell it to the guy. Police raids were an ever-present threat at Dad's stores, so I knew Mike had to be careful about what he sold and to whom.

There was a constant stream of customers, men of all ages, coming through those front doors. Some were heterosexual, some were bisexual or gay. Their ethnicity and socioeconomic status ran the gamut. Most surprising for me, there were also *women* who

The Princess of 42nd Street

showed up to partake in porn. Some were barely over 18 and most ventured in with excited boyfriends.

Some fathers would bring their sons in on their 18th birthdays. *Was this how they taught them about sex?* No wonder so many men were such bad lovers. Learning from porn is the worst way to learn about sex, unless a guy is watching lesbian porn. Now, there he will learn a thing or two about how to satisfy a lady!

I was also surprised at the parade of salt-and-pepper-haired businessmen dressed in Givenchy suits who looked like they just stepped from Wall Street to 42nd Street. I was spellbound, too, as cheerful, extremely ordinary-looking couples walked hand-in-hand through the door. And I was curious as solo men looking for a quick self-pleasuring session in the video booth would stop by on the way home from work. Customers would saunter down each aisle, looking at the magazines and paraphernalia, carefully selecting one or two items. Men would pause at the rows of condoms and think carefully about whether to buy ribbed or un-ribbed. Lubricated. Extra snug. Thick or thin. Small, Medium or Max.

The more time I spent around Times Square and 42nd Street, the more I realized that most people who visited my dad's porn shops weren't gross, disgusting or perverted. They were just trying to find ways to explore and fulfill their sexual desires. Our hypocritical, straight-laced, Puritanical society (then and now) didn't allow people a safe, compassionate and understanding space to explore and express these perfectly normal feelings. So, consequently, these feelings were suppressed and forced underground, until indulging in porn became the only realistic outlet.

The time I spent hanging out at the porn shops taught me much more than any psychology, sociology or human sexuality class ever could; in particular, that lots of different people like lots of different kinds of sex, and as long as everyone is of age and having fun, why not make the most of it and enjoy it while you can?

* * *

Even as my own understanding of human sexuality expanded and evolved, I realized that a lot of people considered Dad's business to be selling smut and serving up sleaze, exploiting society's baser instincts in order to line his own pockets. But for us, his family, Dad's businesses represented the public side of Dad's life. Our private life as a family, the life we lived at 37 Harborview West, even though it was often violent, chaotic and confusing, it was still just that—*private*.

But that was about to change in a very shocking and dramatic way as any privacy the Hodas family may have had was ripped to pieces, torn to shreds, as sordid, salacious details (not to mention many outright lies) about our personal lives hit the front pages of the New York and national press, and Martin Hodas, Porno King, became the poster boy for all that was seemingly wrong in America. Meanwhile, we, his children, struggled with learning some hard truths about our father while simultaneously dealing with our lives being put on public display.

Chapter Ten

The Feds Close In
1971-1972

While Dad was busy living his public life on 42nd Street as New York's "King of Porn" and his private life as a Long Island husband and father to a seriously mentally ill wife and four angry teen and preteen kids, other forces--darker, more sinister, and more malevolent--were at work behind the scenes, scheming to bring him down, like a noose tightening. Dad had pissed off a lot of powerful people in his time—good guys, bad guys and wise guys, among others.

Looking back, there were signs that something big was brewing for years, something that had Dad smack-dab at its center. For example, when I was a teenager and we were living in Lawrence, all our phones were routinely tapped. It was so obvious that our phones were being tapped that we made a joke of it and would talk directly to whoever might be listening in:

"Oh, hey, Joni, wait a minute, I think I just heard a guy breathing. Let's say hello to the FBI agent on the other end!"

Or, "Hang on, Joey, I just heard someone else come on the line. Let's wait until they get situated so they can hear us clearly...All right, guy, can you hear us over there? Is it okay with you if we continue our conversation now?"

This went on for years, and we always tried to make light of it, turning it into something fun, and funny, even though at times it felt scary and horrible, having our lives invaded in such a personal and intimate way. Mom and Dad both knew this was going on, too, and they always joked about it as well. Maybe they thought we would find it less disturbing and less upsetting if they acted like it was no big deal. But it *was* a big deal. Other kids didn't have to deal with having their phones tapped; this wasn't a normal life, as far as I was concerned.

Meanwhile, Dad wasn't exactly making the kinds of choices that would help his own cause. Quite the opposite, in fact. Most of the other men involved in the sex and porn business kept as low a profile as possible, but not Dad. Ever the showman, Marty Hodas thrived on attention and did everything he could to promote and publicize himself and his businesses. In 1969, he was the subject of a colorful profile piece in *The New York Times*. Soon after, he began appearing on the radio and TV shows like *The David Susskind Show*, and wrote letters to the newspapers moaning that the cops and the media were treating him unfairly. Martin Hodas became more than a public figure; he became fodder for the media, especially in and around New York City.

By happily assuming the mantel of "the public face of porn" when so many of his colleagues were determined to fly under the radar, Dad must have realized that he was making himself an obvious target for the mayor, the DA, the police, the vice squad and any other group that had a motive, political or otherwise, to score brownie points with the public by cracking down on sleaze and "cleaning up Times Square." Dad must have known, but did he care? In his ruthless quest for notoriety, did he ever once consider what effect this would have on his wife and children?

Maybe to Dad, his time in the limelight, his role center stage, was more important than the family at home who loved him. And this made me the angriest. Power and money were more important to him than we were. Mom was mentally ill; he was just selfish, not to mention a degree psychotic and narcissistic.

The authorities responded to Dad raising his own public profile by coming down on him hard. It started small, with minor harassments and inconveniences, and slowly, steadily, escalated from there. For example, Dad started getting phone calls at home at 1:00 and 2:00 in the morning telling him he had to come into the city right away because the cops had raided one of his stores and found something illegal (something, Dad later insisted, the cops themselves had planted there).

Or they would claim the curtains in one of his stores were a fire hazard, and he'd have to prove to them that they weren't by attempting to set them on fire. Dad believed that a lot of the pressure on him was coming from the assistant district attorney at the time, John H. Jacobs, who saw cleaning up 42nd Street as a way to further his own political ambitions.

A significant turning point in this high-stakes game of cat-and-mouse came on January 20, 1970, when the Commission of Investigation of the State of New York subpoenaed Dad to appear before the commission as part of an investigation into, "… organized crime and racketeering with reference to the extent to which business enterprises connected with or related in any manner to the production, distribution, sale, rental or exhibition of sexually-oriented material or films, as well as the manufacture, sale, or lease of equipment used in what is commonly known as the 'peep show' have been infiltrated or are controlled or carried on by elements of organized criminal groups, and the extent to which such activities involve criminal conduct and violation of the laws of the State of New York."

In other words, the commission was investigating the extent of the mob's involvement in, and influence over the pornography and adult entertainment business. The commission also claimed that Dad had failed to report a significant portion of his income from his peep machines, and therefore they also subpoenaed all his books and financial records for 1968 and 1969, looking for (and no doubt hoping to find) any discrepancies.

Dad never spoke to us about his testimony before the commission (he rarely talked to us about anything going on in his "public life," even as we suffered the terrible fallout from his actions), but records show that he vehemently denied any failure to declare income and equally vehemently denied having any association with organized crime.

Dad must have seen that the writing was on the wall by this point, but perhaps his hubris allowed him to feel he was untouchable. But if the powers-that-be couldn't bring him down one way (obscenity, mob ties, etc.), they would certainly look for another (tax evasion). That's how the feds finally broke Al Capone, after all.

The State of New York Commission of Investigation claimed that by the middle of 1970, there were 1,000 peep show machines in Manhattan alone, and that Dad owned 350 while the rest—650—were owned by the Mafia. Dad, for his part, always acknowledged that he supplied peep show machines to adult bookstores that were owned by the mob, but he always, always insisted that he never gave the mob any payoffs in exchange for protection.

Instead, Dad had connections with the Westies, a tough,

predominantly Irish gang from Hell's Kitchen, and in particular, a loan shark named Whitey who helped keep Dad safe from the Mafia. The exact nature of the relationship between Dad and Whitey wasn't revealed to me until many years later, when Dad told me all the details just three days before he died in 2014.

Still, the authorities were relentless in their righteous zeal to purge Times Square and 42nd Street of their unsavory elements, and in mid-1971, the tall, handsome, patrician New York Mayor John V. Lindsay established a new task force dubbed the "Times Square Inspectional Task Force," organized under the auspices of the city's Commission of Investigation and headed by no-nonsense, tough-as-nails Police Commissioner Patrick V. Murphy. Whatever the task force's noble goals, in reality, the crackdown translated into frequent police raids on live sex shows and adult bookstores, arresting and taking into custody unwitting employees and throwing them in jail on various obscenity charges.

For Dad, the task force crackdown was more annoying than impactful, and while he felt the heat, he was able to continue growing and expanding his businesses relatively unencumbered. By this time, he owned and oversaw a conglomerate of 12 interrelated and interconnected businesses that included not only peep shows and peep show machine repair but also massage parlors, adult bookstores, photo studios, adult film production, distribution and exhibition, mail order and property ownership and leasing.

However, the porn world's relative stability was shattered on June 28th, 1971, when the head of the Colombo crime family, Joseph Colombo, Sr., was shot in the head and critically wounded at a rally for Italian-American civil rights at New York's Columbus Circle. Although the young black man who pulled the trigger was killed on the spot (but till this day no one knows whether it was by police, by Colombo's bodyguards or by someone else), many people believed the man who was really behind the shooting was Gambino family member Joe Gallo (the same Joe Gallo who engaged in the "jukebox jumping war" with Dad years earlier).

Joseph Colombo survived the shooting but remained essentially comatose for seven years, until he died in 1978. Following the 1971 shooting, an all-out Mafia war erupted among New York's "Five Families," a war in which Times Square and 42nd Street represented

The Princess of 42nd Street

valuable real estate, prime turf worth fighting for, and Dad, like so many others, would be caught in the crossfire, quite literally, in this case.

I'm not able to track down many details about what actually happened, and Dad never discussed the incident with us, but in the autumn of 1971, three Mafia enforcers allegedly came to Dad's office on 42nd Street and demanded protection money and a cut from his profits. Dad refused, so the hoods drew their guns and fired several shots at Dad, all of which missed. Then, with the help of his bodyguard and another guy, Dad tossed two of the three mobsters down the back stairs of his office while the third guy ran away. Could it have happened like that? That's what the media reported at the time, even though it sounds completely unrealistic. We'll never know now, but it seems probable that someone did at least take a shot at Dad during that period.

* * *

As Dad's world darkened, I placed my own focus elsewhere. I couldn't bear to see what was happening to my family, so I spent as little time at home as possible. I spent as much time as I could with Joey, the gorgeous boy who would become the first of my three husbands. I was 13 when we met; he was 15, and I fell for him—hard. What I had felt for Knuckles was nothing compared to the depth and maturity of my feelings for Joey.

Joey used to come and meet me outside Lawrence High when my classes let out at the end of the day, and we'd go back to my house (where my mom was mostly in her room at this point), or his family's house in Brooklyn, Marine Park, to be exact. Many times I would cut school and hitchhike on the Belt Parkway or through Far Rockaway, which was very dangerous, but I didn't care, because nothing would keep me from seeing Joey.

We would party in Joey's basement, smoke pot, listen to music—The Grateful Dead, Marshall Tucker Band, Santana—and play beneath his psychedelic "blacklight" posters. (For those of you too young to remember the '70s, blacklight posters were large wall posters with wild, intricate designs and vivid, fluorescent colors that appeared to shimmer and move when viewed in black light and that looked amazing if you were high.)

Joey lived with his parents and two younger brothers. His three older sisters were already married and out of the house. When Joey's mother found out who my father was, that was it—especially when she started reading in the newspapers all about "The Porno King." She would make me sit outside in Joey's green van while he was eating dinner. The irony is, once Joey's mother invited me inside and got to know me, we became very close and had a great relationship for years.

On days Joey didn't pick me up from school, I'd hitchhike to Brooklyn to see him, and we'd hang out with our friends Brian, Cary and Earl, but it was always clear that Joey was the leader of the pack. As crazy as I was for him and as much as we fooled around, I told him I wouldn't sleep with him until he told me that he loved me more than he loved his ex-girlfriend, Cora.

I was 14 and a half and had been dating Joey for about a year when it finally happened. I was upstairs in my bedroom, sitting on my bed, reading a letter that Joey had written me. He signed the letter, "Love, Joey." This was it! This was what I had been waiting for! I jumped off the bed and flew down the stairs, screaming to my mother and anyone else who was there, "Mom, Mom, Joey says he loves me!"

Sometime after that letter, after we had talked it over, Joey and I decided to make love. I skipped school and we went to his house to have some privacy. We were up in his bedroom because I didn't want my first time to happen in a basement. I lay back on his bed and there was a warm breeze floating through the window, just as there had been when I'd been intimate with Knuckles for the first time.

Joey sensed my nervousness and wanted to help. "Here, have some beer," he said, gently lifting my head and bringing the can of Budweiser to my lips. I've never much liked the taste of beer, but I did as he said and took three small sips. Even just those few sips had me feeling warm and tipsy.

After playing with my body and getting me so ready, I was nearly begging him. "Okay, when I count to three, I want you to really, really relax," he said. I took a deep breath, tried to relax, and then... then he took me to heaven. My first time was wonderful! I was so happy to have lost my virginity to someone I loved and who loved me in return. I was pleased and surprised that it didn't hurt, as I had expected. Maybe I had broken my hymen horseback riding? The first time we made love was beautiful, but as time went on and we had more practice, it just got better and better!

Joey taught me how to explore his body and mine. And boy, did he have a great body! Wow! He was so gentle and patient, postponing his own pleasure for so long, that when we finally came together, it was amazing.

After that, Joey and I had sex at every opportunity. We were insatiable; nothing could stop us. Even if we were with our friends, they had to wait until Joey and I were done having sex before we could all hang out or go do something. In fact, that is exactly how I met my dear friend Hannah. After Joey and I finished one of our "sessions," we came out of Cary's bedroom and there was Hannah, standing in the hallway, having heard all the hoopla. She gave me a wink and a sly smile and we have been friends ever since.

Given how "busy" Joey and I were between the sheets, it's probably not surprising that soon, my family found out about it. Joey and I were at my house in Lawrence, having sex in the basement when my cousin Kenny, who was visiting, heard what we were doing and told Mom. I thought she'd be upset or angry to think that her 14-year-old daughter was sexually active, but instead, she was absolutely wonderful. She was so cool with it, but she did say that if I was going to be having sex, I needed to be on the pill. So she took me to my first gynecologist appointment, which was rough, to say the least. I was not prepared for this experience, and as the doctor had me up on the table spreading my legs, I freaked out, reaching for the walls and scraping the paint off with my fingernails, feeling everything get hot and dark and then... I must have fainted. I blacked out, and the next thing I knew, Mom was in the room beside me and the doctor was nervous and shaking, saying, "I didn't do anything, Mrs. Hodas, I swear I didn't do anything..."

As the doctor tried to complete the exam, Mom stayed with me, holding my hand, talking to me, and trying to keep my mind occupied and not focusing on what was happening between my legs. Bizarrely, Mom started to ramble, and suddenly she revealed that *she* had baked those pot brownies that Risa, her friend Joyce, and I had found in the kitchen before one of my parents' parties a year earlier, the brownies that had made Risa and Joyce so sick. So now I knew for sure who baked those pot brownies! *Okay, Mom! Thanks for sharing that, I guess.*

Overall, that was a strange day, but I have always been so grateful to my mom for being cool about me having sex, and for making sex something wonderful and beautiful. This is one of my happiest memories of her, and one of the greatest gifts she gave me—a positive, healthy, joyful attitude toward sex. I was so fortunate in this regard. One thing she did say, though, was that we couldn't tell Dad that I was having sex with Joey, because he would freak out. *Mom, like I didn't know that? You better believe I'm not planning to tell Dad.*

During that time, I still had a nightly curfew of 11:30 p.m. One evening, Joey and I had driven in his green van to a town called Breezy Point where it was free to park at the beach at sunset. There was a bed that Joey built in the back of his van, so we had sex there and then fell asleep. I woke up suddenly, looked at my watch, and saw that it was already past 11:30. "Joey! Joey! Get up!" I yelled, shaking his shoulder. "You've got to get me back home—now!" I shook him and shook him but he just moaned sleepily and turned over, burying his head in the pillow. "Joey, c'mon—please!"

Now, at 14 I had never taken a driving lesson in my life, and I certainly didn't have a license, but I figured, how hard could driving be? In my desperation, I grabbed Joey's keys, climbed behind the wheel, started the van, and attempted to drive away. *Smash—smash—smash—smash—smash—*I sideswiped five cars before I even maneuvered out of the parking lot. "What the hell are you doing?" Joey shouted, bolting upright from the bed behind me, suddenly wide awake.

"You wouldn't get up, and I need to get home!" I yelled over my shoulder. Joey quickly got behind the wheel and we sped back to my house in Lawrence. Dad was there waiting for me and he was livid. "Where the hell have you been?" he screamed, his face red and puffy. "You were supposed to be back here at 11:30!"

As he read me the riot act, I couldn't help thinking, "What's the big deal? What's so special about 11:30? What could I be doing at 11:30 that I couldn't do at 10:15?"

Because Dad had such a raunchy attitude toward sex, he couldn't understand the tender, innocent, sexual love that Joey and I shared. Maybe because Dad's mind was always in the gutter, he saw everything in those terms. For example, one time David, a friend of mine, came over to our house to swim. I was dating Joey, and David

The Princess of 42nd Street

was just a platonic friend—there was nothing going on between us. David had taken a shower after swimming and was in the bathroom with his pants on, blow-drying his hair. I was sitting on the counter across from him and we were just talking. The door was wide open. But then Dad came by and saw us and started screaming at me, "You whore! You're nothing but a cheap whore! Get the hell out of there!" I was so embarrassed and confused, I didn't know what to say to David, and he ducked out quickly, not making eye contact.

* * *

As time went by, I found myself withdrawing more and more from my family. If it hadn't been for Risa, Rhonda and Jarrett, I might have left it all behind, run away with Joey to Haight-Ashbury and become a flower child. Our dream was to hop in his van and just drive cross-country, never looking back. (A dream that did partially come true a few years later). I dreamed of freedom with Joey, far from the hell of 37 Harborview West. I loved Joey, but I hated everything else—my school, my home, the way I looked, my life.

As I mentioned earlier, if Joey didn't pick me up, I would hitchhike to see him in Brooklyn. Hitchhiking was never a safe endeavor, but it was especially risky in New York. One time a guy picked me up in Far Rockaway and took me to the marina in Brooklyn, where he forced me to get out of his car and into a boat that was dry-docked. When I realized what he intended to do to me, I kneed him in the groin, jumped off the boat, and ran away as fast as I could. I was terrified, but that didn't stop me from hitchhiking. I was willing to do anything, even risk my life, as long as it got me out of the house and closer to Joey.

I tried to lose myself in sex, drugs and music. I took to stealing money and drugs from my parents, and I'm certain they never noticed. On Friday nights, when Mom was downstairs watching TV or in her studio, and Dad was out swinging or whatever he did for fun in those days, I would sneak into their bedroom and take $100 bills from the little armoire where Dad would stuff them, and I would steal quarter bags of cocaine from behind the bar downstairs. Thousands of dollars of it every week. Then Joey and I would go to our friend Billy's house in Brooklyn, hang out in his attic, listen to music, and do lines of coke, getting so high that nothing else mattered.

Sometimes there were girls at these parties, girlfriends of all the guys we knew, but these girls never liked me. They resented me because they said I "came from money," and I hated that they thought I was just another stuck-up girl from the Five Towns. They never even gave me a chance. In my mind, I was still "Fat Moley," just a working-class girl from Bethpage and Malverne; I hadn't been raised in the lap of luxury, even though we were wealthy now.

While I was trying to escape my own life, the police were continuing to make Dad's life a misery. On January 27th, 1972, NYPD officers once again raided one of Dad's offices, only this time, they found in one of his desk drawers a handwritten note that said:

John gets $4,000 each week until $100,000 is received. Thereafter he receives $1,000 each week for the rest of the year. All new stores, Marty puts up to 50% cash with John and we are partners. Marty assumes all responsibility for running the stores.

The police insisted that "John" was in fact John (Sonny) Franzese, a Colombo crime family lieutenant who'd been involved in the Times Square porn business since 1967.

"John' isn't Sonny Franzese!" Dad swore to us, to the media, to anyone who would listen. "John is John, my business partner! You know, John!" The man Dad referred to was a guy we all knew well, a long-time partner who'd been in Dad's inner circle for years and who in fact later worked with my brother.

"The police are trying to frame me," Dad protested. "They have been after me for years. They will do anything, tell any lie, to link me to the mob. But I swear to you, this note is for an innocent business deal, nothing more."

Did I believe Dad? Frankly, I did, but who the hell knew anymore? I wasn't yet 15 years old and I felt like I'd hit rock bottom. Of course, I had no idea that the feds and the gutter press were just getting started, and that much worse was still to come.

Chapter Eleven

Moon Landings, Marty Hodas and the Daily News
1972

After the cops raided Dad's office in January 1972 and found the handwritten note supposedly referring to Dad brokering a business deal with Colombo family capo John "Sonny" Franzese, the intense pressure on him and on his businesses increased exponentially. That spring, it was decreed that the peep show booths inside adult bookstores in New York City were required to carry a city amusement license. That may sound harmless enough—it was just a little piece of paper, after all—but in practical terms, this gave the NYPD even greater scope to crack down on the porn shops on 42nd Street and bust whomever looked at them sideways or happened to get in their way.

In April, Dad was caught up, along with 11 other men and six corporations, in a massive sting and indicted for "wholesale promotion of obscene material." The numerous charges included 11 individual felony counts against Dad, and each of the counts carried a potential sentence of seven years in jail.

Meanwhile, in May, a massage parlor on 42nd Street called "The Palace" was firebombed and burned to the ground, causing several injuries but no deaths. In July of that year, another 42nd Street massage parlor, the French Model Studio, also burned down as the result of a suspicious fire. What made these events significant to us was that the Palace and the French Model Studio had stood on either side of a massage parlor called the Geisha House. Dad didn't own the Geisha House—it was owned by two of Dad's associates, Jerome "Jerry" Gomberg and George "Georgie" Kaplan—but Dad did own the building in which the Geisha was located, making him Gomberg and Kaplan's landlord. Both fires appeared to be arson, and word on the street was that the DA was going to try to pin the crime on Gomberg, Kaplan and Dad and indict all three on charges of arson.

Dad rarely talked to us about what was going on in his world, and, most of the time, we were too terrified to ask. We just knew things were really, really bad. Almost every day he arrived home from work crashing down from a massive cocaine or Black Beauty high, raging at anyone and anything unfortunate enough to get between him and the first of his several glasses of vodka on ice that he needed in order to "relax."

Meanwhile, Mom had descended so deeply into her mental illness that she had lost almost all touch with reality. In the rare moments that she was awake and aware, she would dose herself with Percocet or Codeine until she passed out and then sleep the rest of the day. I was 15, dealing with typical 15-year-old stuff, trying to negotiate my freshman year of high school, keep up my grades and enjoy my first serious boyfriend (Joey) and our mind-blowing sex, while simultaneously doing whatever I could to care for, protect and provide for my younger siblings.

At times, the whole situation just felt unbearable. I don't think my siblings understood the pain I felt in my heart for them at that time. This is a burden I still carry inside me today, wishing so badly that I could make things better for them, and then feeling such a sense of loss and failure when I can't.

As an example of what I mean, one day, a bunch of kids was over to our house, mostly friends of Risa, Rhonda and Jarrett, and there was nothing to eat for dinner. It was the weekend and the housekeeper was off. I had to ask Mom for money so I could go get food. She had been in bed for months at this point, completely cut off from us and from the world around her.

I gathered up all my courage and knocked on her door. "Mom?" I called softly. No answer. "Mom?" I called louder. "It's Romola." I heard her moan. "Mom, I need some money. We're hungry and I need to get dinner."

There were sounds of the bed creaking and then her bare feet padding across the carpet. After a few moments, she opened the door, wearing a short, see-through negligee with nothing on underneath. Her filthy red hair was matted with knots and her teeth were green

The Princess of 42nd Street

around the gums. She had a big wad of bills clutched tightly in her fist and suddenly she started tossing the money—$100 bills—down the stairs and screaming, "ALLLLL you want me for is MY MONEYYYYYY!!!

I looked downstairs and it was like someone had busted open a piñata full of cash as the kids scrambled all over each other, fighting to grab the bills and stuff them in their pockets.

"Don't any of you dare touch a thing!" I screamed down to them. "Leave that money alone!" I tried to calm Mom down, saying very gently, "Mom, it's okay. Let's just get you back into your room. You're nude, Mom. Let's get you back to bed."

Once I had her back in the room and settled on her bed, I ran downstairs, gathered up all the bills I could and snatched the rest out of everyone's dirty little hands. I brought the money back upstairs, took one bill off the top so I could get dinner, and handed the rest to Mom, who looked at me vacantly, slumped on her bed with her eyes not focusing.

That night, I was glad the kids had food, but I couldn't eat a thing. My stomach was knotted shut with shame, grief, and sorrow.

Scenes like this became so common. Invariably, I would have to muster all my strength to knock on that door and face whatever version of my mother was waiting for me on the other side. "Mom, it's raining. How are we going to get to school?" "Mom, we need money for lunch."

And then her voice sounding like the Wicked Witch of the West, rising from beneath the covers in the dark depths of that room: "Whhhhaaattt the hell do you want from me?"

Sometimes I found the nerve to go into her room, and when I saw the pitiful state she was in, I would say, "Mom, let's change your underwear. And let's brush your teeth, okay?" It was heartbreaking to watch what was happening to her, and Dad was no help at all.

One of the most disturbing incidents of all came once when Joey was over. I needed the car and had to ask Mom for the keys. I knocked on her door very gingerly, and when I thought I heard her answer, I went in. "Mom," I said gently. "Can I borrow the car?"

Suddenly, she just freaked out. "YOU are NOT touching MMMMMMMMYYYYY car!" she shrieked.

"All right, I won't," I said, shaken, and hurried back to my room, where Joey was waiting, looking confused.

The moment I sat down on that damn green couch/daybed, suddenly there Mom was, standing in my doorway, in a see-through negligee with nothing underneath, smiling and swinging the car keys from her finger. "Romola, hon, when you go out, can you bring me back a pack of cigarettes?" she asked, just as sweet and kind as could be.

And then, I don't know, something happened because I blacked out. I just blacked out, the same as I had when Dad had me come see his live sex show and again when the man tried to kidnap me at fat camp. The next thing I remember, Joey was slapping my face saying, "Wake up, Romola! Wake up!" This was just such a weird, frightening, embarrassing situation.

And yet there were those other times, when Mom was in the manic phase of her bipolar disease, she'd be painting and sculpting and taking art classes, fully engaged with the world. I remember one time, during one of her good periods, sitting with her at the bar downstairs and saying, "Mom, I hope you don't mind me trying to take care of the kids when you're not well."

"Of course not, darling," she said, taking a drag on her Virginia Slim. But I knew differently. I felt like she secretly hated me, and she would later even accuse me of trying to "steal her children."

Why does it have to be like this? I thought in despair. *Why can't I have a normal mom and a normal life, whatever that may be? I know my friends have problems in their families too, but nothing like this.*

* * *

As if things weren't bad enough, Dad went and got himself arrested. (This was while both the obscenity case and the arson case were still pending.) The arrest came as a shock to the rest of us, but apparently not to Dad. (It would have been nice of him to have given us a head's up, but hey, "concern for others" was never one of Dad's strong points.)

The police had been tailing Dad for weeks, months, maybe longer, desperate to pin something on him and collect the prize for having brought down the Porno King of New York. Not only that, Dad had a contact on the police force who told him straight out,

The Princess of 42nd Street

"Marty, you're the number-one target in New York. You *will* be arrested. You know why? Because the guy who arrests you will get his name in the paper."

On November 29th, a cop wearing a wire met with Dad in his office. Apparently, there was some discussion about Dad paying the cop $50 a week in exchange for police "protection" from the mob, but the cops were clear that if there had been an offer of a bribe, Dad had retracted it. But then, according to the cop, Dad leaned forward and whispered softly in the cop's ear so the wire couldn't capture it, "If you're straight, I'll take care of you; don't worry." When the cop asked who would pay him, the cop alleged that Dad outlined the name "Jerry" on the palm of his hand.

Dad, of course, denied this story completely and claimed the whole thing was another setup. But now, the die had been cast, and what happened next was probably inevitable.

It was 1:30 a.m. Friday, December 1st, 1972, just a week after we'd spent a very somber Thanksgiving, when the police came banging on the door of our house at 37 Harborview West in Lawrence, shattering the silence of a cold, early winter morning and scaring the living shit out of us. "Open up! Police! Open up!" they shouted.

Dad hurried downstairs and opened the door, cursing up a storm and demanding to know what the hell was going on. One cop grabbed Dad's shoulder and held him in place while the other slapped the handcuffs around his wrists.

"Martin Hodas, you are under arrest on suspicion of bribing a police officer," the cop said calmly. "You have the right to remain silent. Anything you say can and will be used against you in a court of law. You have the right to speak to an attorney, and to have an attorney present during any questioning..."

By this time, we had all stumbled out of our bedrooms, rubbing our eyes and catching our breath, still clad in nightgowns and pajamas, wondering if this were all some terrible dream. The kids huddled with Mom at the top of the stairs, looking shocked and terrified, while I went down to try to help Dad in any way I could.

"Don't worry, Paula, everything will be okay," Dad insisted, trying to sound calm as the cops spun him around and marched him out the door. "It's just a misunderstanding. I'll be back before you know it, hon. It's nothing." I stood at the front door helplessly, face pressed to the glass, watching as they bundled him into the back seat of the squad car and slammed the door shut just as a few loose snowflakes began to sift from the sky.

There was nothing I could do; there was nothing any of us could do, as the cops transported Dad to the city jail, a hellhole nicknamed "The Tombs," where he would spend the night surrounded by drug dealers, car thieves, rapists and pimps, in a damp, cramped, 6' x 6' cell where, he later told us, he couldn't even see the ceiling because it was so covered in cockroaches, and where rats raced over his feet as he tried to sleep

The cops busted Dad for allegedly bribing the cop in his office two days earlier, and even though the police said that Dad "retracted" his bribe, they arrested him for supposedly making the offer in the first place. Dad made the $35,000 bail and was back home later that morning. As soon as I got home from school that afternoon, I was all over him, asking him what the hell happened, but he just said everything was okay and I shouldn't worry. But I worried. I really, really worried. This time he was only gone a few hours. What would happen to us, to the family, if Dad got sent away long-term?

All in all, from 1970 to 1973, Dad would be arrested 12 times, mostly on misdemeanor obscenity charges, and indicted for felonies on three different occasions. All these charges were ultimately dismissed, except for the indictment for arson in the second degree related to the Palace and French Model Studio massage parlor fires, an indictment that finally came down in the summer of 1973 and which I'll describe in more detail later.

* * *

The first human being to set foot on the moon—Neil Armstrong—took his historic steps on July 20th, 1969, and the whole world held its collective breath, witnessing this extraordinary event. By 1972, just three years later, a sixth crew of three brave men was in the middle of making that epic journey once again, and while the level of international excitement didn't rival that which had surrounded Armstrong's Apollo 11 mission, another moon landing was big, big news for media outlets everywhere. Everywhere, that is, except for New York City's morning tabloid, the *Daily News*.

You wanna guess what they had splashed in a stark, giant font across their front page on that historic day of Monday, December 11, 1972? It was: HOW PORNO KING BUILT EMPIRE. Only beneath that, in a significantly smaller typeface, almost as an afterthought, did it mention that "Astros to Land on Moon Today."

Yep, my dad, Martin J. Hodas, was a bigger story than the moon landing. Can you imagine what *that* did to his gigantic ego? It had such an effect on him that even more than 40 years later, when interviewed for a podcast, Dad mentioned this, still not believing the *Daily News* made him bigger than the moon landing.

What you probably can't imagine is the effect these stories had on the private lives of my siblings and myself, just ordinary Long Island schoolkids. In short, all hell broke loose.

I didn't see the first of the four articles, written by reporter William Sherman, until I got home from school that day, and what I read shocked me. *What the fuck? Who is this person Sherman's writing about?* I certainly didn't recognize this "Marty Hodas" character as my father. Mr. Sherman's writing style could be best described as Damon Runyon meets Mickey Spillane as he related Dad "fondling a fistful of 20s he pulled out of a drawer and munching on almond crescent cookies," having a "deep nasal whine," and attributing quotes to Dad with terrible grammar, such as "That don't make me a criminal."

The article began on the top of the newspaper's page three, beneath the headline, "That 42d St. Porn? Well, Meet the King," and was accompanied by a photo of Dad in his office and a map of Times Square, showing the area from 42nd to 51st Streets and from Sixth to Eighth Avenues, with black dots marking the locations of businesses that Dad owned or controlled.

The paper shook in my hands as I read: *"In a few short years, Martin (King of Porno) Hodas managed to pyramid a handful of standup viewing machines and a few storefronts into the largest single empire of pornography and sex shows in the Times Square area,"* the article began. *"What follows, the result of a month-long probe by* The News, *is the start of a four-part series detailing the life style of the man himself, his multimillion-dollar corporate structure, his links to the Mafia, and what may be the beginning of the end of the Hodas Porno Empire."*

Oh my God! What the hell is this shit? I raced through the article, which was full of claims that Dad was the head of a vast empire made up of massage parlors, bookstores, peep show machines and other businesses, that he grossed more than $13,000,000 annually, and that he dealt directly with the heads of the Mafia crime families, accepting money from them in exchange for protection. There was only one very small line in the whole article reminding the reader that, as the Manhattan Assistant District Attorney John Jacobs himself acknowledged, there was no direct evidence of any kind that linked Dad to any Mafia family.

I continued reading. *"Hodas packs a gun—he has a license for it. His associates include a bodyguard and partner in the massage parlor business, George (KO) Kaplan, a former prize fighter, also out of Brownsville, and a man who has a long arrest record but few convictions. He was, in fact, arrested twice for murder, but he beat both charges—one in 1968 at arraignment in Manhattan, and the second this year on appeal.*

'I needed George to bodyguard for me because they shot at me, they threatened my family,' Hodas said, 'but he's really a gentle guy, a nice guy.'

And Hodas himself is described as a 'nice guy' by his neighbors in Lawrence, where he lives with his wife, Paula, and his children, Garrett, 8, (Who did Sherman interview? Someone who didn't even know my brother's name is "Jarrett," not "Garrett?") *"Rhonda, 10, Risa, 13, and Romola, 15.*

They live in a house far removed from the seedy shops in Times Square where Hodas has his machines. Valued at $175,000, the house borders directly on Bannister Creek, across from the Lawrence Yacht Club. There is a full-size swimming pool where the neighborhood kids frolic in the summer, a cabana and steam room in the shape of a pagoda, and a basement filled with jukeboxes, pinball machines and other adult toys."

I was shocked. First of all, the article was filled with numerous factual errors. (Dad didn't drive to work at 9:00 a.m., he took the 8:20 train every morning; Dad's desk was wooden, not Formica; we had one dog, not two. Those were just a few of many I could list.) Maybe it seems small or petty to focus on what could be perceived as minor incorrect details, but in my mind, then and now, if Sherman got so

The Princess of 42nd Street

many simple, basic facts wrong, how could anyone know if *anything* he had written was true?

Moreover, what right did this William Sherman have to blast our private lives all over the news? Did anybody really need to know how much my parents' house was worth, or the shape of our steam room? That detail was of public importance *how*, exactly? And the bags we received full of horrible letters asking my mother why she stayed with my dad. Some came with rosaries and prayers for my mom. This certainly didn't help her mental and emotional state.

Sherman went on to describe Dad as a "devoted family man" involved with Little League, and quoted comments from an unnamed "neighbor" who mentioned, *"There's that big safe in the basement... he tells the kids he keeps candy in it."* (We all knew who this "neighbor" was—Mrs. X., who was always drunk and came to my parents' swinger parties, where she indulged in her fair share of drink, drugs and extramarital sex. Mom told us that Mrs. X. had wanted to engage in a foursome made up of her and her husband with Mom and Dad, but Dad said no. He wasn't interested in Mrs. X. because she was flat-chested—he preferred big boobs. So we surmised that Mrs. X. talked to the papers as an act of revenge for Dad's rejection.)

The article continued, *"Hodas talked about his home life the other day and his face lit up when he mentioned his kids, his gerbils, and 'my dogs. I really like dogs. I've got two of them, Tiny and Meetzo,' he said."*

Ummm, yeah, Mr. Sherman, I wished I could say to him. We don't have two dogs. Haven't for quite some time. And who the hell has gerbils? We certainly didn't. Did you really talk to Martin Hodas? Or is most of this just a work of fiction, invented to sell papers to naïve and unsuspecting readers?

The next three *Daily News* articles, published on Tuesday, Wednesday and Thursday of that miserable middle week of December, 1972, were no better than the first, full of lies, innuendoes and salacious headlines: "The King Harvests Lush Pornfield: Quarters Build Peep Empire," "Mafia Declares War but Porn King Survives," and "Knights in Blue Crumbling Porn King's Castle."

Unsurprisingly, the articles also featured more examples of Sherman's breathless, penny-dreadful prose that put 1950s' pulp fiction writers to shame: *"It is dark and a rancid odor hangs in the close atmosphere in the back room of 210 W. 42nd St. The only light comes from blurred, red light bulbs shining 'occupied' on top of a long line of wooden closets against the walls.*

Behind the closet doors, some of the patrons are groaning and panting while viewing pornographic, and sometimes absurd combinations of men, women and animals on peep show screens."

How did Sherman know what was on the loops? Did he go into the booths himself and watch the films as part of his "research?" Perhaps he did. Both my parents always swore to us that Dad never dealt in any porn that involved children or animals, but there is no way to know for sure now, so many years later.

* * *

Unusual for Dad, he did talk to us after the first *Daily News* articles appeared, and he swore up and down that none of it was true; he never spoke to William Sherman, was never interviewed in his office, and the reporter made up all the quotes he claimed came from Dad. Dad never explained where the *Daily News* got the photo of him sitting behind his desk, though, although I suppose that could have come from anywhere.

And, as always, Dad absolutely insisted that the articles' primary assertion—that he was making payoffs to the mob in exchange for protection—was patently untrue. He certainly wasn't making weekly payments to the Colombo family, as Sherman stated. As Dad explained it, the mobsters always respected him. He had told them, "I'll never pay you for protection. The only way you'll get my money is if you kill me."

So instead of giving them money, he gave them valuable business information. He taught them how to do what he did and be successful, how to open adult bookstores, how to make and distribute porno films. In other words, Dad's compromise was that he didn't pay the mob; he made himself useful to the mob—useful enough to keep alive.

Moreover, Dad had the Westies, the Irish mob, looking out for him, which meant he could deal with the Italian Mafia on his own terms, without the life-threatening dangers of finding himself in the Mafia's "debt."

My brother, Jarrett, has verified this. Many years later, Jarrett spoke with one of the Italian mobsters from that time period who told him how much the mob admired Dad for being so brave and not giving in to extortion and instead helping them establish their own foothold in porn-related businesses.

Personally, I believed my Dad back then, maybe because I wanted and needed to believe my Dad, needed to believe that he wasn't deep in the pockets of the Colombo crime family. Still, I couldn't handle the *Daily News* articles and the way they defamed my father and my family. My Dad was a terrible father, and yet I felt an intense need to support and defend him. So I used the only tool available to a 15-year-old high school student: I sat down and wrote Mr. William Sherman a letter. Nothing mattered more to me than giving that asshole a piece of my mind.

Dad when he was younger, about 24

Mom and Dad, 1963

The Princess of 42nd Street

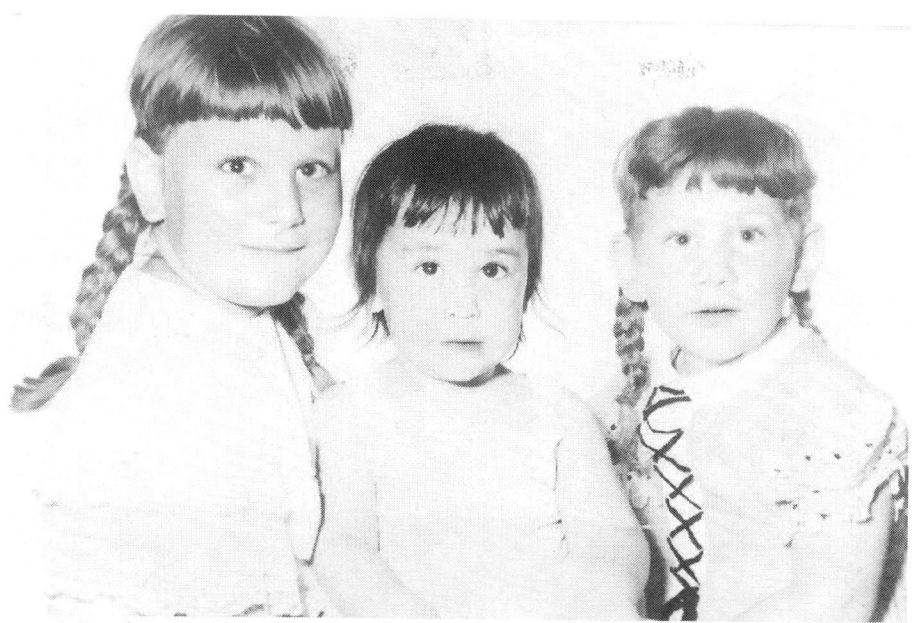

My sisters and I. Romola(6), Rhonda(2), and Risa(4) in 1963

Knuckles and me at camp, I am 13. 1970

Romola Hodas

Me and Grandma Mina circa 1972

Mom was happy when we first moved into Lawrence in 1972

The Princess of 42nd Street

Jarrett & Me in Puerto Rico in 1973

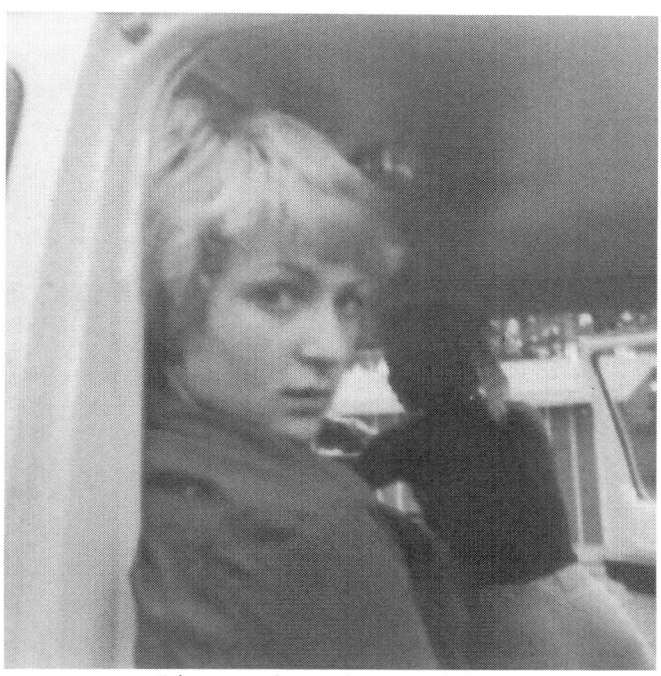

Diane at Start Center, 1974

Romola Hodas

Mom and Dad's 20th Anniversary, 1976

Joni and me having dinner in California, 1976

The Princess of 42nd Street

Me, Joey, Sue and Bob at a Grateful Dead concert in 1977

Booths in one of Dad's stores circa mid 70's

Romola Hodas

Alex (Risa's husband), Mom and Risa 1976

My family in the den, getting ready for my wedding.
Jarrett, Me, Mom, Dad, Rhonda, Risa Oct. 6th, 1979

The Princess of 42nd Street

Joey and Romola's wedding

Liz and Me dancing at my wedding, 1979

Hannah and me at Risa's wedding, 1982

Carlos and me at his apartment on 86th St., 1983

The Princess of 42nd Street

Risa with her father in law, Izzy and her daughters, Leyna and Veronica, 1990

Dad and me on my 40th Birthday, 1997

Chapter Twelve

Romola Strikes Back
1972-1973

(Letter from Romola Hodas, age 15, to reporter William Sherman of the Daily News)

December 12, 1972

Dear Mr. Sherman,
    I can no longer sit and read the horrible lies which you are allowing to be written in the paper about my father. How dare you accuse him of saying things which you have no justice to print!
    My father is a good man, with a good vocabulary. The things which you write sound as though he never passed the sixth grade.
    Are you afraid of losing your job by printing the truth? Why is everyone out to make big names for themselves? Do you know the danger my younger brother and sisters have put in front of them? I'm afraid to see them go to school now, in fear they might not return. How could you be so heartless, not to think of what you are putting my family through? How do you have the nerve to print our names and address? You cannot imagine the letters we got and we'll still receive.
    There is so much proof of what you and other "big men" are saying, that my father is no more dishonest than myself. I cannot say you because you showed me what kind of "man" you are.
    I can only be happy as to know I can hold my head high in front of the people in school. They too know the garbage which is written in your newspaper. Where is the justice in this world? To know I am being brought up with men like you and the DA makes me sick. Do you have kids, Mr. Sherman? Do you know what my parents are

going through when each and every one of us go out my front door? Where is your heart? How come, on the front page, there can't be the truth AS YOU KNOW IT!

I know my family is only six people out of many, why should you care what burdens are on their backs, when you are getting money for your sick, stomach-turning lies?

Do you think only lies sell the paper? Millions would be surprised to see good written about someone.

Where did you get your information, Mr. Sherman? My wonderful neighbor? There's more to write about her and her husband—the truth—that would shock you out of your mind!! Where do you come off to quote my father in saying things which he never said? You, my dear man, are the "sadist." You are dishonorable and corrupt.

I hope my brother and sisters don't have to go through hell like I am, knowing the trash which is being told. Instead of lying and making matters worse, why not show the public the truth, REAL facts of my father's honesty? You come show me my 40-foot boat and our big safe. See how "unmatchy" my house is. Why not come watch my father's ball games! You think he has time with all this on his mind to be in the Little League? If you have questions—ask my father, not the neighbors. Are you so ignorant to know you're wrong? So heartless to put children in danger? What hurts me is you know you are wrong. You know what you wrote is first degree trash, why not make it known to others? The people who need to know! Lie a little more Mr. Sherman, you seem to be good at it, tell the public from higher means you discovered the truth of the man. If you're half human you'll care and not put this letter in the trash with a laugh. Don't say to yourself here's a child sticking up for her father like any girl. The fact is we both know what I'm saying is the truth. Be a man, be human, show a few people this got into the mess you call your brain.

If you think I am rude, disgusted is a better word. My father is a good, hard-working, honorable man. I know and you know it, isn't it time everyone else knew it? Come back down off your ego trip and help make things better. No more than the truth is what I beg you to write.

Romola Hodas

By the way—we only have one dog.

* * *

When I read this letter today, as an adult, I am both shocked by what I wrote then and deeply touched. I was so fierce, so steadfast and righteous in my support and defense of my dad. I knew, even then, that Dad wasn't always a good person and didn't always do good things. After all, this is the same father who wrote me that letter when I wasn't even ten years old, the one that said, "At this moment, I do not care for you as a person. I am not obligated to do anything I don't want to do for anyone."

He had been so cruel to me for so many years, and yet the love I felt for him surpassed all that. He was my dad, and I wouldn't let anyone—the press, the police, the DA, the Mafia—say terrible things about him or hurt him in any way. I was determined to protect my family, no matter what, even though I was just a kid myself and should have been the one being protected.

Even before the final of the four *Daily News* articles appeared in print, my life turned upside down. Now, not only was I this fat, freaky, ugly girl, I was also the daughter of New York's King of Porn, which made me the object of torment and abuse, especially from one of my teachers and some of my peers. I was stared at, sniggered at, called horrible names, chosen last in gym class. Some kids rode by our house on their bikes one day and shouted that someone found porno pictures of my mother having sex with a horse.

Kids who'd been my friends, some for several years, were now forbidden to see me, and their parents no longer allowed me into their homes because of who my father was. I felt like a leper, like Typhoid Mary, someone carrying a horrible, deadly, contagious disease who might infect anyone I came into contact with. It's like my Dad's business had rubbed off on me, and people now saw me as an outcast, a smutty, damaged, dirty girl.

My first-period science teacher, Miss Goldberg, was one of the worst offenders. "So, Romola, why don't you tell the class—do you *really* have a trap door in the floor of your basement?" she asked, in class, the morning after the first *Daily News* article ran. "And is it true there's a safe inside there that's full of money and candy?" The other kids all laughed as I shrank down in my seat, my face burning red. I wished more than anything that I could just go up and punch that smirk right off her face or, even better, have the floor suddenly open up beneath me and swallow me whole.

First period every day that week started with Miss Goldberg grilling me on what she had read in the papers the day before. Instead of discussing sedimentary rocks, or cumulus clouds, or stalactites versus stalagmites, or any of the other material we were supposed to be covering in class, Miss Goldberg devoted a large portion of time to discussing Porno King Marty Hodas, and whatever new and salacious things she had just read about us in the gutter press.

At first I wanted to scream at her and defend Dad as best I could, but after a few days I began to detach, dissociating myself from my feelings and from what was happening around me. I moved through my days like a zombie, trying to get from place to place without thinking or feeling anything. When I look back on that time now, I get so angry. How could a teacher do that to a student? Where was Miss Goldberg's compassion? Her decency, her care and concern for a vulnerable student in pain? People like her have no business teaching children, in my opinion. If it hadn't been for the love and support from Joey and from my friend Liz, I don't know how I would have gotten through that time.

When I first met Liz, I couldn't have imagined the role she would play in my life. Miraculously, I had been invited to a party in Atlantic Beach and was planning to go spend the night at the home of one of my parents' friends after the party. My parents were hosting one of their own wild swinger parties that night and they didn't want us at home. (They *finally* made a good decision about having us kids out of the house when their craziness took place—unfortunately, their good judgment didn't last long.)

Anyway, after the party in Atlantic Beach was over, I announced that I was taking a cab to North Woodmere and asked if anyone else needed a ride. A girl named Liz said that she lived in North Woodmere and would be happy to split the fare. Well, either I had lost the address of my parents' friends or I couldn't read my own handwriting because I ended up spending the night at Liz's house, thereby beginning a 40-plus-year friendship that's had more than its share of ups and downs.

Liz had long blonde hair and wore her jeans at her hips, with a big brown leather belt resting right on her hipbones. She also had an older brother with some very good-looking friends. When I first went to her house, I was amazed that she had such a feminine, girly bedroom, so different from mine! She had a chandelier and frilly things and furniture in shades of cream, soft pink and white. Sometimes we'd climb out of her bedroom window and sit on the roof, smoking cigarettes or pot and talking until all hours of the night. Elton John's "Your Song" had just come out and it became our song. We thought it was so pretty.

One thing that created a bond between us was that we both had moms who were sick. Liz's mom had early-stage MS, so she was in bed a lot, just like my mom. And like my mom, Liz's mom was prone to sudden, unexpected attacks of rage. One time I remember being in the car with them when Liz's mom stopped the car, jumped into the back seat, and started hitting her. And like me, she also had a dad who caused the family a lot of grief.

Liz and I became fast friends. We would cut school and go to Greenwich Village to get Indian food. Her grandparents lived there so she knew the area well. When things were at their worst, Liz and I would cut school and pretend she was taking care of me. And as I look back on it today, I see that she *was* taking care of me, and I was taking care of her, too, which is what created such a strong bond between us. She would phone the school psychologist, Dr. Orlophsky, and say, "Romola isn't feeling well today. She's not going to be able to make it to class."

"Okay, Liz, thanks for letting us know," the doctor replied. "And take good care of her, okay?"

"Oh, I will, I will."

As soon as she hung up, on went the baby oil, up went the sun visors, Liz lit up a cigarette and we lay out for hours, soaking up the sun, smoking pot and laughing our asses off!

But it wasn't all fun and games. Another time, Liz and I were invited to a friend's bar mitzvah and I ended up sitting on the steps outside Temple Israel, shaking and crying my eyes out. I was so scared and I wanted to feel safe. I felt like I was so fat and deformed, and my life was such a terrible mess. Liz tried to comfort me, but there was really nothing she could say or do to help. Although being at Liz's house, flirting with her brother's friends and getting high, certainly offered some pleasant escape when I wasn't with Joey.

The few friends I cultivated during this difficult period were a lifesaver, not just Liz but also Stacey and Pam. On rare occasions, my friends would come over to the house, but I tried to avoid that because I never knew what state Mom would be in. It was embarrassing to have her always in the bedroom with the door closed, but it was much worse to have the door open and her sitting on the bed in a see-through nightgown, wearing big bangles stacked up and down her arms from wrist to elbow and her fingers covered with rings, and my friends actually thinking she was different and cool. They had no idea that I was waiting, and fearing, her turning into the scary mom, a change that could happen on a moment's notice. Not many people saw *that* mom, fortunately. Liz did, though, so she understood a lot about my situation with Mom.

One of my strongest memories of that time is having Liz and Stacey over at my house and Stacey saying, "Come on, I want you to hear these albums of my brother's." Stacey had two older brothers. I didn't want to hear some nerdy music, but when she played the Allman Brothers' *Eat a Peach* and Santana's *Abraxas*, I was blown away. Every song was amazing! I feel so lucky to have been born when I was and grown up hearing the most incredible music.

In addition to Stacey, Pam and Liz, I also hung out with Joni and Ronnie and sometimes Linda. We all had some shit going on in our families that made us feel weird, like outcasts, but that also brought us together because each understood something about what the other person was going through. One of my friends had a horrible, scary bitch of a mother who caused her so much pain. Another friend had a brother with emotional issues and the mother forbade anyone in the family to talk about him. This attitude was more common back in the '70s, that you don't air the family business in public. But this created a heavy burden for so many kids, this feeling that you carried inside you a terrible, horrible dark secret and you couldn't tell anyone about it, not even your closest friends. Teaching children not to trust anyone, even those they are closest to, creates a lifetime of problems with trust, intimacy, relationships, and so much more.

Fortunately for me, I had this core group of friends I hung out with. We all had family problems, but some of us, especially me and Liz, could talk about those things with each other, which, when I look back, may be one of the only things that kept me sane during that very, very difficult period.

***

On June 9th, 1973, I celebrated my milestone birthday and turned Sweet 16. My parents arranged a huge party for me at Goldie's, a longtime Five Towns institution, a family-style Italian restaurant known for its live jazz music, great calamari and questionable décor—the walls were covered with garish paintings of clowns—happy clowns, sad clowns, creepy clowns, you name it—over 50 clown portraits in all.

Every town has its own version of Goldie's, a favorite local gathering place where people celebrate birthdays and anniversaries and first communions, and where the Lions Club, the Kiwanis and the Knights of Columbus hold their monthly meetings in a room in back. Overseeing it all was "Goldie" himself, aka Alberto Francisco Natale Occhiuzzo, a WWII Air Force veteran who founded Goldie's in 1962 and ran it, along with several generations of his family.

Goldie's was also where Mom and Dad used to hang out with their swinger pals, until Mom had had enough of Dad embarrassing her in front of other people and she started staying home with her "backaches." But Dad kept going to Goldie's on his own and, for some reason, maybe because it was at Goldie's, he decided to invite all his swinger friends to my Sweet 16 party. *Why?* I wondered. *Why do they need to be here? This is supposed to be* my *party.*

My friends were there too, Joey and Ronnie and Joni, but so many people—my friends and my parents' friends—were stoned out of their minds on coke, and it got pretty crazy. The house band was playing "Dancing in the Moonlight" by King Harvest and I danced with Joey and watched my friends laughing their heads off and singing along with the band. Everyone seemed to be having a great time except me. I excused myself, said I was going to the bathroom or out for a cigarette, and went and sat on the steps outside the restaurant, listening to the noise and the partying going on behind me.

I'm finally 16, I told myself. *In two years, I'll be 18 and a legal adult. Joey and I could just hop in his van, run away to the West Coast, and leave all this behind.* The thought was so very tempting. *But what about Risa, Rhonda and Jarrett? How could I leave them behind? I could never be happy if I knew they were still trapped here with Mom and Dad, living like this while I was free.*

Chapter Thirteen

Marty Beats the Rap—This Time, At Least
1973

The police considered Dad, along with his colleagues George Kaplan and Jerry Gomberg, prime suspects in the firebombing of the two 42nd Street massage parlors—the Palace and the French Model Studio, because Kaplan and Gomberg owned the Geisha, the massage parlor that was located in the middle between the Palace and the French Model Studio, and Dad owned the building that housed the Geisha.

To provide some background, there was a bit of a "massage parlor" price war going on at that time of the firebombing. The standard price for a 15-minute "massage" was $15. (How intimate the "massage" became was open to negotiation, although actual sex cost extra, and was always negotiated separately, and off the books.)

But then some parlors started lowering their prices to $12 to generate more business. Rival parlors then lowered their prices as well in order to stay competitive. So, some parlors then lowered their prices even further to $10, and even all the way down to $7.50 for a massage.

It was impossible to keep a massage parlor business viable at these low rates, so it was thought that the fires were set in order to send a message that "you better keep your prices in line with your competition, or else face the consequences."

After keeping Dad waiting, along with George and Jerry, for more than a year, on July 13th, 1973, Manhattan District Attorney Joey S. Hogan announced that all three men were being indicted for the massage parlor fires. The four-count indictment against Dad included two counts of arson in the second degree and two counts of criminal mischief, and he faced up to 25 years in prison if convicted on all four counts. Dad was arraigned and pled not guilty. Bail was set at $50,000 and a hearing was set for July.

This indictment was really quite extraordinary, if you think about it. Assistant District Attorney John Jacobs, the man Dad always felt had it in for him, even said that they did not believe that Dad, George or Jerry had personally set the fires. Even so, all three were indicted for arson. To Dad, this seemed a clear case of the feds trying to pin "something" on him, no matter how nebulous. If they couldn't show that Marty Hodas was giving payoffs to the mob, then they'd find something else to accuse him of—in this case, arson.

The media, too, was not immune from allowing Dad's reputation as the Porn King to obscure the facts. The *New York Times*'s lede in the next day's report on the indictments was, "Martin J. Hodas, reportedly the head of a multimillion-dollar pornography operation here who has been closely linked with organized crime, was indicted yesterday on charges of fire-bombing two rival 'massage parlors' in the Times Square area."

If Dad was indicted on arson, why did it matter how much his business was worth? And "closely linked" with organized crime? That had not been proven. Clearly, it was going to be hard for Dad and his friends to get a fair trial before a jury of their peers, based on the aggressive, ambitious reach of the DA's office combined with the sleazy Porn King picture the media continually painted of Marty Hodas.

And just how did the indictment go down at home, you may wonder? I have no idea. By the age of 16 I was done with fat camp, but that summer, my parents sent me to Blue Mountain Camp in Pennsylvania, where my most enduring memory is of the open concrete showers, where I felt very fat and exposed, showering in front of so many other, slimmer girls. At least I was away from the hell of home for a few brief months.

My younger siblings were also away at camp that summer, and that may have been a very good thing, because on August 6th, something truly terrifying happened at home and, unbelievably, it ended up with Dad charged with yet another crime. The poor guy really couldn't catch a break.

It was around 5:00 a.m. that Monday morning and Mom and Dad were home alone, sleeping upstairs in their bedroom, when Dad woke to find a large man in the room with them, hovering over Mom, leaning in as if about to attack her. Dad bolted upright, reached for the 22-caliber Beretta automatic handgun that he kept in the nightstand for protection and shouted, "Stop—I've got a gun."

The guy turned and lunged at Dad. Dad fired one shot but missed the guy. Mom woke up screaming when she heard the shot. "Paula—stay here!" Dad shouted as the intruder ran out of the room and downstairs. Dad ran after him, firing another shot, which also missed. The intruder ran out the back door with Dad following. The neighbors heard the commotion and called the police.

When Dad went back inside, Mom was in shock. Dad tried to calm her down and then noticed that his dresser had been ransacked. Dad checked and it looked like the guy had stolen some of Dad's jewelry, about $1,500 worth. Was this a straight-up burglary? Or was it something else—a message from the mob, perhaps—disguised as a burglary? Our neighbors, the Slofkis, were awakened by all the noise and found that they'd been robbed, too, apparently by the same burglar, of $800 cash, a mink jacket and a man's watch.

Most amazingly, rather than putting their efforts into catching the perp, the cops instead turned around and arrested Dad, charging him with illegal possession of a loaded firearm. Dad had had a legal permit to carry a gun, but that had been revoked the previous December, when Dad was arrested for allegedly bribing the police officer.

Dad always knew there were people out to get him, so he kept the gun to protect himself, Mom and us. And thank God he did! Who knows how different this incident might have been had Dad been unarmed when he confronted the burglar.

Dad pled not guilty at his arraignment. The media, of course, couldn't resist highlighting Dad's reputation when reporting the incident. The *New York Times*, in particular, couldn't resist mentioning that "Mr. Hodas, who, the police say, has connections with the Joseph Colombo Mafia family..."

* * *

When Risa, Rhonda, Jarrett and I got home from camp that summer, tension in the house was at an all-time high, but we still didn't know a lot about what was going on with Dad at work and in the courts. I started tenth grade at Lawrence High that fall, but studying and academics were the last thing on my mind. Dad was potentially facing a long prison sentence; Mom was upstairs in her room slowly killing herself; my siblings were running crazy. Meanwhile, I was stealing money and drugs from my parents, skipping school and hitchhiking to Brooklyn to be with Joey as much as possible. My life was unbearable, and I was acting out in any way I could, trying to lose myself in pot or coke or sex, anything to get a break from the fear and stress and the constant reminders that I was the eldest daughter of New York's "King of Porn."

On December 16th, 1973, the trial finally began for my father and his two colleagues, George Kaplan and Jerry Gomberg, on the charges of firebombing the Times Square massage parlors a year and a half earlier. Dad must have been so nervous sitting in court, waiting for the proceeding to start—he faced up to 25 years in prison if convicted on all four courts. Even today, I can't imagine what it would have done to our family if he'd been sentenced to 25 years, or sentenced to ten years, or even just five. Mom was much too ill to take care of us, and there was only so much I could do as a 16-year-old high school student.

Amazingly (or maybe not so amazing, since if you've read this far in the book, you understand my dysfunctional family pretty well by now), we never discussed any of these things at home, within the family. When Dad went to court each morning that week, it was like he was heading off to work on an ordinary workday, and we all went off to school as usual. At night, we ate dinner mostly without Mom or Dad at the table, and did our homework as usual, counting the days until the upcoming winter break.

When I think back to that time now, it makes me so sad. I wish so badly that my parents had shared with us some of what was really going on in their lives, in all our lives, really, since these things affected everyone. I'd like to think I'd have had much more empathy and compassion for my parents, and I certainly wouldn't have been acting out and fighting and arguing with them all the time like I was. I would have understood more about why Dad was such a nightmare when he came home each night, why he was so angry, stressed and bad-tempered, and why Mom was so sad and disconnected. I would have done so much more to help and support them, had I known.

The trial lasted seven days. During the trial, the owner of the

The Princess of 42nd Street

French Model Studio massage parlor, a man named Nick Valentine, testified that shortly after the fire at the Palace, he met with Dad, George and Jerry at a local hotel and was warned by Dad that if he didn't bring the cost of a 15-minute massage at his establishment back up in line with the competition, the French Model Studio would suffer the same fate as the Palace. Valentine testified that he agreed in the meeting to bring up his prices but then did not follow through on his promise.

Also testifying during the trial were the two men actually accused of setting the fires, Dexter Morton and Earl Jones, who claimed they'd been offered a total of $300 to set the fires. Interestingly, while both Morton and Jones had been arrested for committing the two arson attacks, neither man was ever brought to trial.

After seven days of testimony, in the end, it only took the jury four hours of deliberation to reach their verdict. George Kaplan and Jerry Gomberg were both convicted on two counts of arson, and each faced up to 50 years in prison. (They ended up serving eight years each.)

I can't imagine what must have been going through Dad's mind as he waited to hear his fate. And then the jury returned its verdict. NOT GUILTY. Dad was acquitted of all charges. It was over! He walked out of court a free man that day, Saturday, December 22nd, 1973. We may have been Jewish, but I can't imagine anyone receiving a better Christmas gift than that.

Afterwards, defense lawyer Seymour Detsky spoke to the press and maintained that the prosecution's case "relied on testimony of convicted perjurers, forgers, arsonists, and (sic) man who stated he was at one time an inmate of an insane asylum." Moreover, each of the principal witnesses had criminal records that were brought out in court. Detsky added, "And these were the incredible people whom the jury chose to believe."

I can't say I even remember any specific details of that cold winter Saturday when Dad came home to share his great news, but I do remember, so fondly, the trip to Puerto Rico we all took as a family over the Christmas/New Year's break. We had so much fun! We went swimming and sight-seeing and rode donkeys. Mom and Dad were actually getting along, enjoying the trip and each other. Dad so wanted the trip to be perfect for us. In fact, when the rain wouldn't stop in Puerto Rico, Dad chartered a small plane to fly us over to St. John's, where the weather was better.

As we sat in the beautiful Caribbean restaurant on the final night of our trip, I thought about everything we'd been through as a family. *This could be a turning point*, I thought. *Maybe the worst is now over and things will get better. The Hodas family came close to losing everything. Mom and Dad, especially Dad, must realize that; he must realize how lucky he is, how he could have ended up like George and Jerry, facing possible decades in prison. Dad will try harder for us now. I will try harder. We all will. I pray that things will be different when we get home.*

Chapter Fourteen

The Joyful Relief of Reform School
1974

Remember what I wrote, that I thought my family was about to turn a corner and have a fresh start, how things would get better and we'd all try harder? Yeah, well, I could *not* have been more wrong about that, because the next thing I knew, my parents had had enough of me, so they decided to ship me off to reform school to get me out of the house and out of their hair.

What precipitated this was me skipping school every day for two weeks straight to be with Joey. When my parents found out about all the classes I had missed, they could have grounded me, or they could have forbidden me to see Joey, whom they considered a bad influence. That's what most parents would have done, but not mine. No, my parents took me to Family Court and had me sentenced to juvenile detention, for what they said would be one month.

At the time, I assumed that sending me away had been Dad's idea, to punish me and to get me away from Joey. But Risa later told me that she thought it was Mom who wanted me out of the house because she was so tired of my behavior and of me constantly fighting both her and Dad. Risa said that Dad actually didn't want to send me away, but it was Mom who insisted.

In any event, I just went numb when I found out. I couldn't believe this was happening to me. At least I would only be gone a month, I reminded myself, and then I could get back to school, Joey, my friends and my regular life in Lawrence. I told myself to look at this like an enforced vacation. *And who doesn't occasionally enjoy a change of scenery?*

I think I have since blocked out everything that happened

between the time I was sentenced to detention and the day I actually arrived there because I don't remember anything about that time period. The only distinct thing I recall is Mom dropping me off at the START Center on Staten Island and whispering in my ear, "Romola, you're going to be here for longer than a month."

What? How much longer? What are you saying? What have you done to me? She knew how long it could be, but she chose not to tell me, maybe because she realized I'd never agree to go if I knew how long I *really* might be there.

* * *

Mom and I arrived at the START Center by driving up a long driveway and through a gate that opened to let us in. The center itself was housed in a big, sprawling, one-story contemporary brick building. At first glance, it didn't appear sterile or intimidating like a prison; it looked more like a modern school.

The interior of the building included a large living room with couches (I later learned this was where we'd have group therapy) and a restaurant-style kitchen. The eating area looked like a diner with large windows and eight booths against the windows. Down the corridor were the bedrooms, two girls to a room, that resembled dorm rooms, only slightly larger. Bathrooms were at the end of the corridor, and there was a special room, long and narrow, with lighted mirrors for putting on make-up.

Just outside the building were picnic tables and a trampoline, and also a separate one-room building where classes were held. *This doesn't look too bad*, I thought. *Especially if I have to be here for more than a month...*

At the center there were about 30 other girls, my fellow "detainees," along with several counselors. While Mom was still there with me, Lois, one of the counselors, explained that the program I was in had a three-tier process for completion, and you had to pass each level before you could advance to the next. The program was individualized, so it would be up to me in terms of how long it would take to get through each tier. *Yeah,* I was thinking, *I'm going to be here* way *longer than one month...*

While I was at the center, I would be taking classes toward my

The Princess of 42nd Street

GED, *attending group therapy, and would also have a job. Complete my GED? That means never going back to Lawrence High to finish school, missing the senior prom, never being in class again with my friends...* I was devastated. Scared shitless. So much of my everyday life was disappearing right before my eyes.

That first night at the center, I went to bed feeling terrified, lost and confused. *Why did Mom and Dad do this to me? Am I really such a terrible daughter? When will I get to see Risa, Rhonda and Jarrett again? I already miss Joey so much, and it's still only day one.* I barely slept that night, tossing and turning in this strange bed in this strange room, feeling so abandoned and alone.

And then something amazing happened as I settled in to life at the START Center. I actually began to enjoy it. Don't get me wrong—this was no country club or ladies' finishing school. I was living side-by-side with prostitutes, heroin addicts, truants and juvenile delinquents, girls who'd hustled on the streets, who'd witnessed terrible things. There were some tough girls, and given my privileged upbringing on Long Island, it was like I'd come to them from another planet.

But I learned to hold my own and really stand up for myself. Early on, I was in the make-up room fixing my make-up when two black girls, Vicky and Lorraine, came in and started angrily harassing me about my looks, my hair, my money. They knew, as everyone did, that I was the daughter of Marty Hodas, New York's King of Porn. I finally turned away from the mirror and said, "Look, what do you have against me? I can't help where I come from. I didn't make the money; my parents did. And I can't help that I have long blond hair. This is just who I am. I'm not trying to make you feel bad; this is just my life." After that, we all became friendly.

One of the key elements of the START program was group therapy, which was held five nights a week, Monday through Friday. The sessions were led by Mrs. McFarland, whom we nicknamed "McFoo." Adjacent to the huge living room where group therapy was held was what was known as the "Mad Room." Inside were a set of dummies representing "Mom" and "Dad," and also a baseball bat, which was there so you could work out your aggression and beat up "Mom" and "Dad" during or after a particularly difficult session.

Lots of people loved to take that bat and whack the shit out of

"Mom" and "Dad," but I could never do it. Whatever I felt, whatever emerged during the sessions, I just couldn't bring myself to hurt my parents, even in dummy form.

I remember one girl, tall, muscular, stony-faced, like an Amazon, who came to START after I did. Some of us were scared or intimidated by her, but the miracle of this place, and of McFoo in particular, was that by the end of her first week or two, this young woman was sitting on McFoo's lap like a very large child, smiling and hugging her. It was beautiful to watch, and it showed me in such a real way how love and kindness bring out the best in people.

While I was at START, my family only came to visit me once, and that was for my graduation. Prior to that, we kept in touch via letters and the allotted one phone call per week, so at least I had some contact with home during those sometimes very lonely days.

I found that the more time I spent at the center, the stronger and more confident I became. It was here, during the therapy sessions, that I first really came to understand that I had to take care of myself, that I was only going to have one life as Romola Hodas, and if I had any hope of surviving all the shit my parents had put me through, I had to learn to be kinder to myself, to talk to myself in a gentler and more loving way. There would always be a lot to be miserable about in life; it was up to me to discover what things in life would truly make me happy, and then, once I had identified those things, make sure I pursued them with all my passion and commitment.

I also found myself growing in self-esteem during my time at START. Maybe because I didn't have my dad constantly berating me, calling me fat and telling me I was an imbecile, I began to see myself in a more positive light. The work we were doing at the center— physically, mentally, emotionally—was really grueling, but I was coping okay, and other people, my peers, teachers and counselors, were noticing strong team-building and leadership skills in me.

I was doing great academically in my classes, and everyone was telling me I should become a lawyer. *A lawyer? Me? Well, why not?* To be honest, I hadn't given much thought to what I might do as my future career. I had spent so many years fighting my parents and trying to protect and care for my younger siblings, I rarely even thought about what would happen when we were all grown up and out of the house, and what my life might be like then. I knew I wanted to be with Joey; that was a given. But beyond that, who knew? It was thrilling to finally be able to see an exciting future for myself as a young woman making my own way in the world.

While at the center I grew close to a girl named Karen. She was the "popular girl," a kind of class clown. She gave me a stuffed animal, a little skunk, which I treasured. Sometimes I would go to her room early in the morning and jump into bed with her before we all had to start the day. I had no idea she was a lesbian, not even when she told me, "Romola, I don't have normal relationships with girls." I was like, "What are you talking about? You seem okay to me." I wouldn't have thought less of her for being a lesbian, but I might have stopped jumping into her bed! Eventually, I was made to understand.

Every weekend we had to do chores, mostly cleaning, dusting, vacuuming, washing pots and pans, waxing and unwaxing the floor, really boring, tedious stuff. Occasionally on the weekend we'd have a field trip. I remember one time, we got to take a trip to Greenwich Village and Karen scored some mescaline. "Cleaning will be so much more fun now," she said with a twinkle in her eye.

*　*　*

After I had been at the center for a few months, I was on the trampoline one day with a heavyset girl who fell on top of me and broke my ankle. It hurt like hell! My ankle and calf were placed in a plaster cast up to my knee and I was sent home to heal.

I don't remember much about my time at home, except that I would sneak Joey into the house for visits. Mom would be in her room, Dad at work, and the kids at school. Joey would park his van blocks away from the house and then walk over. We knew this was a huge risk, but we couldn't keep our hands off each other. And more than that, we missed each other terribly.

One vivid memory I have is of an afternoon when I was in Risa and Rhonda's room, resting on Risa's bed. Dad came in with a very serious look on his face, pulled up a chair, and sat down beside me. *This looks bad*, was my immediate thought. *Dad never wants to talk to me like this.*

"Romola, we need to talk about Joey," he began, in a soft, gentle, measured tone I never expected to hear from him.

"What about Joey?" I asked uneasily, pushing myself up in Risa's bed and elevating my cast atop some pillows.

He took a deep breath and sighed. "It's not that I don't like Joey, but you and Joey are so different. You are so much deeper, so much more complex than he is. I just don't think he's right for you."

At first, I was too shocked to speak. *The man who is constantly yelling at me and berating me, now, all of a sudden, he's being kind to me, sitting down like a real parent and talking to me?! What the hell?*

"Dad, I know Joey isn't a rocket scientist, but he's a good, kind, caring person," I argued. "He loves me like crazy, and Joey has so much potential."

Dad rubbed his face, running his hands over his thick, bristly mustache that was now flecked with gray. "Yeah, well, you can't live on potential, Romola. You need to find a man, a nice Jewish man, with a good job, who will support you and give you kids."

"But I want to have a career of my own," I argued. "I don't want to be a housewife with a bunch of kids." And then I told him something I hadn't expected to share with him. "Dad, everybody at START tells me I would make a great lawyer. I'm smart, passionate, and I want to fight for people. Once I've got my GED, I want to study law and psychology." I paused. "Either that or I want to be a social worker, working with troubled teenage girls. I've learned so much at START that I can really relate to people in those situations now."

His face darkened. "I'm raising Jarrett to be a businessman and have a career," he said sternly. "I expect my daughters to marry good Jewish men and have children. That's the future I want for you."

What? I thought back to all the phone calls I had heard Dad make over the years, where he would talk about how important it was to be your own boss and make your own money. He always emphasized having at least two avenues that generated income. I heard this so much while growing up. How was I supposed to know that information was meant for Jarrett, not for me and my sisters? Jarrett had one set of rules to live by, and we had another?

Dad continued, his tone demeaning. "Become a social worker? No way," he scoffed. "First of all, you would make no money at all as a social worker, and knowing you, you would want to help everyone, trying to rescue each and every person who came your way. You'd get too emotionally involved and end up miserable."

I felt crushed. I hadn't realized how much my hopes and dreams meant to me until Dad shot them down. *Dad really does care about me*, I thought. *But he doesn't know me as well as he thinks he does. I'll show him—I'll be really successful someday, as a lawyer or social worker or something else. Then he will really be proud of me.*

I was only home with my broken ankle for two weeks and then I had to return to the START Center. It was bittersweet having to say good-bye to Joey and my siblings, but I was actually looking forward to returning to the center and completing the third tier of my program. Having completed the first two tiers, I had a job there now, doing filing and paperwork for a crazy rabbi at Willowbrook State School, once the largest state-run institution in the US for people with cognitive disabilities. Willowbrook turned out to be a pretty terrible place for its residents. In fact, laws were later enacted to protect people in institutions because of the grotesque and unethical experiments some of the medical staff at Willowbrook performed on their patients. Fortunately, I never witnessed any of that.

While I was working at Willowbrook, one of the residents was a mentally challenged guy in his 40s who used to love helping me do my job. Meanwhile, I was developing all kinds of useful life skills.

I had just gotten the cast off my ankle when some of us chose to go on a two-week survival course in Upstate New York. I wasn't cleared medically to take part because my ankle was still weak—I hadn't had time to rebuild the muscles after so long in the cast—but I begged McFoo to let me take part. Finally, she said yes, after I promised her that I would take a walking stick and go slowly. I kept my word.

One weekend before our trip, we were doing our chores when Karen said to me and Cindy, another of my friends, "Let's do the mescaline I scored in Greenwich Village." We did, and, as expected, cleaning was a breeze that day! I remember being on the swings, laughing and feeling amazing as I sailed higher and higher toward the sky.

I always suspected that Cindy was a bit jealous of Karen, and I guess I was right because Cindy wound up telling McFoo that we'd been tripping on mescaline. Two days later, Karen was gone and I was crushed.

This was right around the time that a new girl, Diane, arrived at the center. Diane was a tall girl with short blonde hair. She was really pretty and she made me laugh. On the third day after Diane arrived, we were all suddenly ordered to the therapy room. Everyone was told to sit in a circle, and they plopped me down in the middle. Diane later told me she was scared shitless, thinking this was how things normally worked at the center!

Suddenly the counselors started interrogating me, their questions coming hard and fast. "Don't you know Karen is a lesbian? Don't you know you should not have taken the drugs she gave you?" they barked at me. My head started spinning and I no longer heard their questions as a lightbulb flicked on: *So* that's *what Karen meant when she said she didn't have normal relationships with girls.* How was I to know? I had always shared a bed with my female friends, Liz, Laurel and others, and it was purely innocent. I couldn't help laughing to myself, even in that stressful moment. It took a while, but I finally got it!

That was the last straw for Karen and she was thrown out of the center. I was so upset because I relied on her so much. She had been a safe place for me, and now she was gone. At least I had Diane, and we became close friends, which we still are today. (Karen and I reconnected about four years ago, but we're not sharing a bed!)

* * *

On the day the survival adventure began, we were dropped off with a pair of group leaders in the Adirondack Mountains for our two-week journey. After hiking for three days, we were told that we would be given a compass and we had to find our way north to the designated destination. This was scary, but also so empowering. Once we got there, we were each given three matches, a sleeping bag, water, and some dehydrated food for dinner, and had to make our way to another certain designated area. Once we reached that area, we only had those three matches to build a fire. If you couldn't get a fire started with three matches, you did not eat that night. Fortunately, I was good at starting a campfire because Joey and I camped a lot.

When I reached my designated area, I was thrilled by what I found. They had chosen a wonderful, magical spot on a narrow peninsula, about 25 feet across, that jutted out about 60 feet into a lake. On this little peninsula was a big pine tree with roots that ran partially aboveground and formed a hole, almost like a basket, directly beneath the tree, which was approximately six feet long, three feet wide, and one foot deep.

The Princess of 42nd Street

Perfect! I gathered enough pine needles to create a soft layer of bedding and then laid my sleeping bag over it. A few feet away, I made my campfire, needing only one of my three matches.

As I cooked my dinner, I could hear some girls crying in the distance. They had used all their matches and failed to start a fire, so now they would have to go to bed cold and hungry. I felt so badly for them, but for me, it was an extraordinary night, curled up in my cozy sleeping bag cradled in the base of a towering tree, inhaling the sharp, deep, relaxing scent of pine needles beneath me.

I crossed my arms behind my head and stared up at the stars dancing across the sky. They were so huge and visible out here, so far from city light, it felt as if I could just reach up and grab one, holding its brightness in the palm of my hand. All the sorrow and struggles of my life felt so far away now, much further away than the stars.

"I'm not Fat Moley," I told myself. "And I'm not a moron. I am not an imbecile. I'm so much more than what my parents have told me I am. It's amazing that I had to be sent away to reform school to finally understand that."

* * *

At the end of the first week of our adventure, there was a food drop. All the food needed to be rehydrated; nothing was edible "as is." The next day we were scheduled to take a canoe trip, but it rained for hours and hours and lots of girls were crying. As we paddled up the river, I thought the rain was kind of cool, pelting our skin and creating a misty fog.

We ended up at a real log cabin with a fireplace and an outhouse. We stayed inside the cabin all day, cooking, staying warm and playing games. It was such a fun and relaxing day and we all seemed to grow closer.

Even better, there had been a boys' survival group that somehow ended up at the same cabin with us. Some of the boys started bothering Diane, so Frank, the counselor from START who accompanied us on our trip, had Diane sleep next to him that night. I was oblivious to the boys and just slept beside one of the girls. Who knows what adventure I might have missed out on!

The day after the canoe trip was devoted to rock climbing.

Everyone was supposed to scale this sheer mountain of rock, but I was excused because my broken ankle hadn't fully healed. I was so happy about that!

So instead of climbing, I sat on top of the mountain, calling out support and cheering on the others as they struggled through the climb. I will never forget Diane being so scared as she scaled the face of the mountain, and me urging her on, saying, "Come on, now, Diane, don't give up! You can do it. Just a few more feet. That's it, now pull yourself up... " I offered her my hand and helped pull her up. She's always thanked me for that, and it felt amazing to know I had the power to help other people, that my words and energy could inspire and empower others.

* * *

After I had been at the START center about six or seven months, I finally completed the third tier of my program and earned my GED with flying colors. I felt really proud because some of the girls had been there over a year. There was a graduation ceremony and program for all of us who were leaving, and for our families. That was the only time my family came to see me at START. As part of the graduation program, we performed skits and songs and other routines for the audience made up of the counselors, the girls who weren't graduating and our families.

Diane was my partner and we did a musical/comedy routine. I lay down on my back with my knees up toward the audience, and Diane sat on top of me, facing the crowd. We had material covering us that looked like a skirt and we sang, "Let Me Entertain You" from the show *Gypsy* with my feet and her hands moving independently, but also somehow in unison. It was hysterical! Diane and I laughed almost as much as the audience did.

It was so poignant to say good-bye to the counselors at START and to all the new friends I'd made. I was glad to be going home at last, but I worried, too. I had changed so much during the past months, had grown and matured and evolved in ways I could hardly imagine. I was calm and confident, feeling better about myself than ever before. But how long could this optimism last, once I was back in the toxic Hodas household?

Chapter Fifteen

The House Burns Up and Marty Goes Down
1974

I graduated from the START Center in August, 1974, at the age of 17. As I had expected, readjusting to life back at home after my time at START was really challenging. I remember feeling like I didn't know my role in the family anymore. Everyone had gotten by without me for all those months; where did I fit in now?

Moreover, I had left home as one person and had returned as someone very different. I was so much more confident now and had much better self-esteem because of how people had treated me at START. There, everybody liked me, supported me and looked up to me. My counselors and peers were always telling me that I could become a lawyer, a social worker or a psychiatrist. Can you imagine how that made me feel, the girl who always saw herself as deformed, fat and awkward? I had always felt like Quasimodo and the Pillsbury Doughboy. When people laughed on the other side of the street, I was sure they were laughing at me. Not feeling like a freak anymore was such a relief.

Since I had earned my GED, which is the equivalent of a high school diploma, the next step for me was college. And I couldn't wait to get there! I applied and was accepted to the C.W. Post Campus of Long Island University (now known as LIU Post) in Brookville, intending to major in psychology and law. I was too late for the fall semester, so I'd be starting classes the following semester, which began in January.

During the time in between, I planned to live at home and work. But before long, I found myself really struggling. I was surrounded by too much pot and other drugs, and I started to feel some of my self-esteem slipping away. Joey and I were fighting a lot, too, which didn't help. It pains me to say it, but I think I had outgrown him while we were apart. I still loved him, and he loved me, but I had matured and changed so much while I was gone, really expanded my ambitions and my horizons, while Joey was still just the same old Joey he'd always been, stuck in the same old place.

I searched for a job but there was really nothing that clicked for me, so Dad put me to work in a store he owned in Manhattan on Sixth Avenue and 42nd Street that sold jeans and other clothing. That's where I was working on December 20th, 1974 when Dad and I took the train home from the city after work one evening and were met at the station in Lawrence by members of the local police and fire department.

"Marty?" the cop said carefully. "We need to speak to you for a moment." They didn't even take us aside but stood right there on the platform, in the middle of all the hustle and bustle of people passing by around us. I knew something terrible must have happened. My heart was racing and my thoughts churning. I worried that Dad was about to be arrested again, but that didn't explain why the fire department was here, too. *Oh my God,* I thought quickly. *Please let my family be okay...*

"Mr. Hodas, there was a fire at your home on Harborview West earlier today. Your wife was badly injured and has been taken to the hospital. No one else was hurt," the cop explained. "Your children are fine."

Dad, in shock, mumbled his thanks and we hurried home to see what was left of the house. When we arrived, we were devastated by the scene that greeted us. The damage was extensive, especially the upstairs, where the fire seemed to have started in Mom's studio. Clearly, the house would not be habitable again for a long time.

My sisters and brother were all home from school when the fire broke out late afternoon. Jarrett saw the smoke and he banged and banged on Mom's door, trying to rouse her from her deep, drugged sleep. Once Mom was up, she stumbled around to every room to make sure the kids got out safe, which was how she ended up trapped in her bedroom.

The firefighters grabbed the diving board that was next to the swimming pool (it was winter, so the pool was closed) and placed it up against the side of the house so she could climb out of the window and slide down to safety. Why didn't the firefighters use a ladder to get Mom down? If they had, she might not have been so badly injured.

Mom suffered horrible, deep scratches on her back, arms and legs because she was only wearing a thin negligee, and the rough, sandy surface of the diving board tore her skin to shreds. Although she wasn't burned, she inhaled a huge amount of ash and soot, and ended up spending two weeks in the hospital recovering.

I was distraught, sifting through the damp rubble that was left of our beloved home. All my childhood toys and mementos were gone, and I searched desperately for my photo albums, scrapbooks, and the book where I kept all my precious keepsakes from Joey.

This fire was even more devastating than it sounds. Mom had actually been in the middle of one of her "manic" phases of creativity before the fire happened, painting and sculpting. She was taking art classes at the Brooklyn Museum and had spent months building an extensive and extraordinary portfolio of breathtaking pieces. In fact, she was preparing for a one-woman show, a major exhibition of the work she'd spent months and years creating, when the fire happened.

Not only was Mom preparing for her art show, she was also preparing to leave Dad. She had fallen in love with Mishu, her art teacher, although I'm not sure if the feelings were mutual. She had even stashed away $300,000 cash in her studio and hidden it from Dad to aid her escape and help her establish a new life, far away from him.

Because the fire started in Mom's studio, almost all her artwork was destroyed, along with the $300,000 cash (although that may have been stolen by the firemen; we aren't sure). Only a few of Mom's pieces that hung on a downstairs wall somehow survived the fire.

I felt so bad for Mom. She'd been broken and bedridden for so long, lost in such a deep, dark world of despair where she literally never saw the light of day, and then, finally, she'd found a ray of hope in her love for Mishu and her passion to make art. I so wanted her to leave Dad, even if it made things harder for us. I wanted her to chase that life of love and joy and freedom that she deserved, because clearly, she would never experience that as long as she stayed with Dad and he was constantly berating her, criticizing her and cutting her down. But now all those hopes and dreams of Mom's were gone, literally reduced to rubble, buried among a pile of smoldering ash.

At first, Dad wondered if the fire could have been the work of the mob, trying yet again to send him a message, but the investigators determined that the fire was accidental in nature and was likely caused by an electrical problem. After the fire, Dad decided to rebuild the house on the exact same spot where it had been. But that would take months, so in the meantime, we moved to a horrible rented house in Atlantic Beach.

Following the fire four days before Christmas, the year 1975 started off on a low note. Mom was still in the hospital recovering and we were sent to Grams in Florida while Dad found us a temporary place to live. We wound up on the other side of the Atlantic Beach Bridge, and boy, did we hate that house! The décor was atrocious—all shiny white wallpaper, and each room had a different theme. The living room had huge red and blue lines traveling up and down the walls, and the bathroom wallpaper featured foot-long, bright red lips. Risa's walls had shiny dots all over them while Rhonda's room featured a comic strip design. Maybe the owners thought this was a cute, funky, whimsical summer house, but for us, it was nothing but a tacky nightmare.

At least things perked up later in January when my first semester of classes started at C.W. Post. I was studying criminal justice and psychology. I loved the classes and, after such a difficult few months after returning from START, I was starting to feel better about myself once again. I moved into the dorm on campus, which I loved, but the mood was darkened by a group of three girls at school who were jealous that I slept with Louie, the guy that every girl wanted to sleep with, and so to get back at me, these girls told Joey and then spread it around college that I slept with Louie and his roommate.

I was furious and made these girls tell Joey that it was all a big lie. I was so embarrassed about being the subject of these nasty rumors. It reminded me of when stories about my dad were spread across the papers. Here we go again, I thought. It was like being back in junior high all over again. I had expected so much more from college students. Joey and I had kind of an open relationship at that time. I felt we needed to explore, but I didn't want to rub it in his face like that.

The Princess of 42nd Street

When Mom finally got out of the hospital, she was worse than ever—angry, depressed, withdrawn. And of course Dad being Dad, he was never going to stay out of trouble for very long. At this point, it had been about a year and a half since Dad was acquitted in the arson case, so it was time for him to be back in the headlines again, for all the wrong reasons.

As you may recall, the IRS had been after Dad for years, going back to when he was subpoenaed to appear (and offer up his financial records) to the Commission of Investigation of the State of New York in 1970. It took until the summer of 1975, but Dad, along with his business partner Herb, was finally indicted on charges of tax evasion going all the way back to 1968. If convicted, Dad faced up to eight years in prison.

Dad's trial began on July 21st, 1975 and lasted four agonizing days. The prosecution presented business records, tax documents, and testimony from accountants. They claimed that Dad actually earned $359,000 in 1968 when he reported that one of his companies, East Coast Cinerama Theater, Inc.'s gross income for the year was only $86,000. The prosecutor, Edward Levitt of the Joint Strike Force Against Organized Crime, accused Dad of keeping a "secret set of books" and said he had only paid $171 in taxes for 1968.

The defense's approach was unorthodox, to say the least. Dad's lawyer, Herbert Kassner, explained that Dad had reported East Coast Cinerama's income accurately and paid the appropriate taxes, after deducting the significant payoffs he had made to an extortionist in order to protect himself from violence, and possible worse extortion, courtesy of the mob.

Dad himself testified on the stand that he had paid up to $5,000 a week to a Times Square bookstore owner whom he called "Benny Glass" and described as a "mob-connected figure" who threatened Dad with violence unless regular payoffs were made. Dad said the total protection payments he made to Mr. Glass amounted to $175,000 in 1968, and he had therefore written off this amount as a deduction on his income tax that year. Hence, Dad insisted, he had not evaded paying any taxes that he was required to pay.

This story was so bizarre, on so many levels. What were Dad and his lawyer thinking? Were they on drugs? First of all, Dad had spent years insisting to everyone—to us, the police, the DA, the media, and anyone who would listen—that he absolutely, positively, never, ever made a payoff to the Mafia. He prided himself on that fact. And yet here he was in open court, testifying under oath, that he made regular large payoffs to a "mob-connected figure" in exchange for protection. What's the difference, ultimately, between the "mob" and a "mob-connected figure?" I guess only Dad could explain that distinction, but as far as I know, he never did. I wish I would have asked Dad about this before he died.

The other thing that was so bizarre about the defense's case was that there has never been a time when the IRS considered extortion payments tax-deductible. Trust me, the best tax lawyer in the world could read the tax code forever and never find a way to make that deduction legitimate. (Maybe for Dad extortion payments were just "the cost of doing business," but you'd have a hard time making that assertion stick.)

What were Dad and his lawyer thinking? In some ways, it was like Dad had just given up. Maybe he was tired of fighting the system that seemed so determined to bring him down. Had he chosen to, he likely could have postponed his court case forever, or at least for quite a bit longer.

Basically, under the then-statute of limitations, the IRS only had five years, or until 1973, to indict Dad for taxes he allegedly failed to pay in 1968. But Dad had signed a waiver back when the investigation first began in order to avoid immediate indictment. This waiver effectively suspended the statute of limitations, so the IRS still had the option to come after him even more than five years after the alleged crime took place.

Dad kept signing those waivers, effectively stalling any prosecution, until 1975, when the IRS again offered him the waiver, but this time, Dad refused to sign. He never explained why, although he did later tell one interviewer, "I just decided that's enough, I'm not signing the waiver anymore." Maybe Dad just got tired of playing games and wanted to get it over with.

In the end, after four days of testimony, the jury deliberated for only four hours before returning the verdict. Dad's partner and co-defendant, Herb, was acquitted. Dad was not so fortunate. I can't imagine what was going through his mind and heart as he stood, took a deep breath, faced the jury of six men and six women, and heard the words: *We find the defendant GUILTY.*

The papers described Dad as "somber but not surprised" when the verdict came in.

Dad faced up to five years in prison for tax evasion and three years for filing false income tax documents with the IRS. It was now the end of July and sentencing wouldn't be until the beginning of September. What a nightmare these next few weeks would be as we all waited to hear Dad's fate.

It might surprise you to know that I didn't blame Dad or the choices he made for putting us in this predicament. Many times in my life I was angry with him, but this wasn't one of those times. Instead I felt sorry for him and what he must have been going through as he faced prison. I also felt sick, overcome with such sadness, and my stomach constantly ached as I counted down the days until he left.

How will we cope without him, I worried, *and without knowing when he'll come home?*

Chapter Sixteen

The Surprising Fun of Prison Camp
1975-1976

Once Dad had been convicted of tax evasion in July, waiting that month and a half for his sentencing was agonizing. We knew he was going away for some time, but we didn't know where, or for how long. It could be up to eight years—a lifetime for a family like ours. Jarrett was only 11; if Dad got eight years, Jarrett would be 19 and out of high school by the time Dad was released. The days seemed to pass so slowly.

Needing a break from the hell going on at home, Joey and I realized our long-time dream in August when we climbed into his brother-in-law's dark orange van and drove cross-country from New York to the West Coast. The walls inside the van were carpeted and there was a bed in back. We bought a small refrigerator and lived on canned tuna and Ritz crackers. I only had $180 in my savings account, so I withdrew it all before the trip.

It was hard convincing my dad to let me go away with Joey for almost three weeks. I mean, he had known we were having sex for five years now, so he reluctantly said yes. I was surprised, to be honest.

We started in New York, and, several days into our trip, I awoke from sleep one morning to the sight of what I thought were gigantic clouds, until I scrambled to the passenger seat to get a better look. "Hey, Joey, check it out," I called to him. "Those aren't clouds, those are snow-capped mountains!" We had reached the Grand Tetons. I had never seen mountains so huge and with snow visible in August.

During those few weeks, we crossed the Midwest and headed toward the West Coast. The Rocky Mountains were amazing, as was Yosemite (where we watched Old Faithful erupt), Salt Lake City, Las

The Princess of 42nd Street

Vegas and the Grand Canyon. The Badlands were one of the most beautiful places we visited, almost scary in a way, with nearly 380,000 square miles of buttes and pinnacles. I believe they shot some of *The Planet of the Apes* and other sci-fi films there, because of how strange, lunar and otherworldly the scenery appeared. Seeing so much natural beauty made me feel like I was free at last.

Having grown up on Long Island, I had never truly grasped the breadth and beauty of this vast country. I was awestruck by the sight of mountains ringed by clouds; small towns of fewer than 100 people; the broad, flat Great Plains with fields and fields of corn, undulating in shades of amber and gold that seemed to unfurl forever; the endless blacktopped highways that cut straight through the dusty heart of the desert.

It felt like all of America was our living room. In Las Vegas, we stayed at a KOA campsite and a woman came up to us and gave us a little booklet of coupons for free food and drink. I'm not sure if she could see how hungry and broke we were, but we were so thankful. We went to the casinos and pretended to play. Waitresses came by, asking us what we were drinking, and we got free booze. And using the coupons, we ate like kings, devouring everything in sight after starving for days!

Joey had an amazing ability to find us incredible places to sleep at night if he didn't want to be in a campsite. I remember going off a side road and reaching an area with a wide, rolling river that was shallow enough that you could see the rocks on the riverbed. We made love and had fallen asleep when all of a sudden there came a thunderous noise. I woke up, looked out the window, and saw a herd of what looked like 40 wild mustangs stampeding past the van! To this day, that remains one of the most magical things I have ever seen. The horses stopped beside the river and drank, bowing their majestic heads to sample the cold, rushing waters.

Another gorgeous destination was Lake Mead, outside of Las Vegas, even though we had some unexpected guests. As night fell and Joey and I were cuddling by the fire, a whole colony of bats flew out of the darkness and surrounded us, darting and flapping around our heads. At first I was scared, but within moments, I was mesmerized.

One night, as Joey and I lay stretched out in the bed in the back of the van after making love, he ran his fingers through my hair and whispered in my ear, "It could be like this all the time, you know. We could go anywhere we want, do anything we want. We don't have to go back to New York."

If only he knew how many times I had thought the same thing myself. It was so tempting, the thought of leaving it all behind—Dad's upcoming sentencing, Mom's bipolar scary mood swings, troubles with the girls from college. "It's my sisters and brother," I explained. "How could I leave them behind? Especially once Dad goes away? Mom won't be able to cope. They'll need me more than ever."

I think Joey understood as he held me close and kissed me. It was a bittersweet trip back to New York, knowing the freedom and opportunity we were leaving behind on the West Coast compared to what awaited us back home.

Joey and I actually ran out of money before we even made it back to New York, and he found a "creative" way to cover those final miles. I was really nervous about how we would get home. In the middle of New Jersey, we stopped at a truck stop. I went inside to use the bathroom. When I came back out, Joey waved me over excitedly and whispered, "Get in the van; get in the van!" I did as he asked, and as we sped back onto the freeway, he explained that he had stolen a tankful of gas while I was inside. *How the hell did he do that?* I wondered. I think that this was a clear sign, more than any other, that our trip had reached its end!

And then, what a letdown it was to arrive home. The energy in the house was heavy, to say the least, and I fell back into the constant dread of wondering what would happen to my dad. But at least I had the memories of a wonderful summer vacation to comfort me in my darkest hours.

* * *

Tension was high on Tuesday, September 9, 1975, as Dad arrived at Federal District Court in Manhattan to receive his sentence for the tax evasion conviction he'd received in July. Judge Charles Metzner sentenced Dad to one year in prison, to be served at Eglin Air Force Base prison camp in Florida. One year! This wasn't as bad as the eight years it could have been, but the thought of even one year without Dad at home seemed terrifying. He was a mean pain in the ass, no doubt, but he also, in his own way, kept the family together, physically, financially, and in other ways. *What will happen to us now?* I wondered. I was sick. I saw the tension in him and that made me feel so bad. *How are we going to get through this horror?*

Before the judge handed down the sentence, Dad was given a chance to speak. He used his platform to take issue with how the police, the court and the media continued to portray him, as the multi-million-dollar "pornography king" with ties to the Mafia. Dad told the judge that he had never distributed hardcore porno films, but still, "they call me a porno king," then added, "I have been made into something that I am not."

Dad's lawyer, Herbert Kassner, emphasized this point as well, noting that the probation report submitted to the court showed the police referring to Dad as "the king of pornography." Kassner also added, "I have seen the virtual destruction of this man and his family." And I doubted that Mr. Kassner knew even half of what we were going through at home!

Kassner also asserted that Dad was the victim of a vendetta pursued by a single policeman, a member of the police's organized crime control bureau. The lawyer asked the judge not to treat Dad like a "porno king," but like "any businessman who has not paid his taxes."

Judge Metzner insisted he was doing exactly that. "I'm still dealing with this as an income tax case," he claimed.

* * *

After Dad's sentencing, I felt like the air had been sucked out of me. Things at home were so painful. Mom was in a fog and my father was so low and depressed, completely different from his usual loud, boisterous self. Dad appealed his conviction, but the appeal failed, and he was ordered to a holding center in New York City before being transferred to the prison camp at Eglin Air Force Base in Florida. I found out years later that his trip to Eglin was filled with terrible incidents, but my parents didn't tell me everything, and even today, I don't know the whole story.

The months leading up to Dad being sent away were unbearable.

Even though I had had a contentious relationship with him since the age of eight, I was so scared and heartbroken. Both Risa and Rhonda seemed happy that Dad was leaving, while Jarrett was just too young to fully understand. I started my second semester at C. W. Post that fall, but it was impossible to concentrate on my studies with everything that was going on in my world.

Joey and I were having problems, even after our wonderful trip across America. I had known deep in my heart that my feelings for him had changed. I just didn't know how to leave him. He was my security blanket, my soft place to fall, my steadfast source of comfort when I was going through hell.

Meanwhile, at college, I was still dealing with the fallout of sleeping with Louie first semester. There were friends at school who stuck up for me and really gave those girls who were harassing me a piece of their mind, but to me, all that was just another distraction, added to the house burning down, staying at the horrible place in Atlantic Beach, and Risa going through hell with her boyfriend, acting out and setting the garage on fire.

Worst of all was Mom, who seemed to have hit a low point yet again. She was drugged up and back in bed, withdrawn from the world, and I was doing all I could not to fight with her. Feeling I had no other choice, I made the very tough decision to drop out of college and get a job. My family needed me, and so I put my education on hold, intending to go back as soon as Dad was home from prison.

The story of how I actually found a job is quite strange. Someone from college had told me that if I went to a certain coffee shop in the garment district and sat there by myself, someone would come up and offer me a job. And don't you know, that is exactly what happened.

I went to that coffee shop as instructed. I ordered some lunch and as the waitress was just finishing cleaning the table, a man came up and asked me if I wanted a job. I was amazed! It worked. I said yes, and so this man, Ted, got me a job in the garment district in Manhattan, working as a secretary at a company called "Ms. Sugar" (a take on the Jewish expression "meshuggener," meaning "someone who is a little bit crazy").

Ted was about 5'8", a chubby, plain-looking guy in his early-to-mid-50s who seemed like a gentleman. For being in the garment industry, he dressed pretty casually, typically in a tan suit. Ted would always take me out to lunch, but then things turned disastrous when he started saying that his wife didn't give him what he needed and that he needed oral sex from me. I suppose he felt I owed him because he had gotten me the job at Ms. Sugar. I should have told him to go see some of my Dad's movies or visit one of his massage parlors!

* * *

Meanwhile, Dad seemed to be settling into his new life as a convicted felon. He sent home the craziest letters from the detention center and later from prison, most of which I didn't get the chance to read until recently, many years later. For example, on July 3rd, 1976, when he was still at the holding center, he wrote a letter to Mom where he described working two hours a day, then working out in the gym in the afternoon, and writing his play after supper. "It is coming along just great," he reassured her. "I have two out of five scenes completed and I just know that I am going to produce it as soon as I get home."

The letter continued, "I don't know what has come over me in the last month or two but I now have a yearning desire to write and create. I have so many ideas for all sorts of media. It's quite possible that the field that I am in has never been exploited as to the writing of material that only a man in my business can accomplish."

A man in his business? Was he going to now start writing porn, instead of just filming, producing and distributing it? In the letter he also talks about writing one-hour TV shows and a book, along with winning awards in Toastmasters and putting on a series of skits. Reading these letters today, I have to ask myself, "Was Dad in prison, or was he on some kind of crazy self-development course?" I did later find out that Eglin was a kind of country club for politicians and white-collar criminals.

And from another letter, dated July 7th: "Dear Paula: Enclosed is a few notes from my play. I have finished it finally. I think it is great." *Of course he did!*

The Dad who comes through in the letters was also surprisingly vulnerable, and, not surprisingly, obsessed with his weight. "A friend of mine just bought me a pair of Bermuda shorts to wear, size 36," he reported. "They fit me fine. A little tight after supper but not too bad. When I came in I was a size 41. When I get to Eglin I'm going to go on a real strict diet and do a lot of running and try to come home at least 35. Even though my waist has gone down considerably, I have not lost too much weight while I've been here. The reason is that I am working out on the weights every day and my body is getting hard and my chest is firming up. The muscles are starting to look like muscles, not fat." *Yep, that sounds like Dad.*

Once Dad was actually transferred to Eglin Air Force Base in Florida, conditions didn't sound too terrible. He had to be up at 5:30 and at work by 7:00. They had him repairing phones and phone equipment. His weight remained a primary concern. In one letter to us kids, he wrote, "I've lost about 12 pounds so far and am trying to lose more but it's a battle as you all must know. No different here than anywhere else. The food is very good. We even have a choice of three desserts at every meal, so as you can understand it's tough to lose."

When I read these letters, I understood that Dad's relentless issues with *my* weight could be traced back to the issues he had with his own weight. I actually felt sorry for him, at least a little bit. Didn't excuse the way he treated me, though.

Dad may have been enjoying his enforced vacation at prison camp, but life at home was hell. By now we had moved back to the rebuilt house at 37 Harborview West, finally saying good-bye to that decorator's nightmare of a rented home in Atlantic Beach. We had the housekeeper to do the housework and cook the meals, but I felt I was in charge of the kids' wellbeing, and it was more than I could handle. Mom was so sick and so crazy. It made me long for the times when she was in a really depressed mood but I was at least able to talk to her, to communicate in some way. There had been times when I would just go in and sit with her in her bathroom and listen to her talk.

To get to her bathroom, you had to walk up the stairs on the peach-colored carpet and open a door. Inside was a huge window with a view of the inlet, the beautiful sky, and the Atlantic Beach Bridge. The bathroom had a huge, green, sunken bathtub so large that six people could easily sit in it at one time. The carpet was light green, and all the fixtures in the house were gold with handles shaped like fish. There were two huge walk-in closets, one for Dad and one for her. On the opposite

The Princess of 42nd Street

side of the closets were huge mirrors and two green sinks. On the wall to the right of them was the green bidet and toilet.

Sometimes, Mom would sit on the toilet in her negligee and I would sit on the edge of the tub and just let her talk. She was so angry and blamed everything on my father. Or she'd want me to hear about the book she read or the movie she saw. Why she had to be on the toilet, I don't know, and it was weird, but at least I had my mother for a while, and I treasured those few, precious moments as if they were jewels. But it was also very disturbing because I knew I was sitting there with someone who was unhinged, someone who had serious mental problems but who just happened to be my mom.

But now, even strange moments like those seemed a million miles away, and Mom and I were fighting a lot. Things came to a head one day when I was at work and I got a frantic phone call from Risa. "Romola! Mom locked herself in her bathroom and she's saying she's going to kill herself. You gotta come home. Please, come home now!"

"Just hang on, Ris, I'll be home as soon as I can," I promised, grabbing my purse and rushing out of the office, yelling to my boss over my shoulder that I had a family emergency. All the way home on the train, I was shaking, terrified of what I'd find once I got there. *Please let Mom be okay*, I prayed. *Please don't let her hurt herself...*

I rushed through the front door, breathless, ran up the stairs to Mom's bedroom, and was met by Mrs. Mendelson, our neighbor who was also somewhat of a friend of Mom's. She too had a difficult husband. He actually brought home his mistress—don't get me started on that. Anyway, she was there, trying to calm Mom down. Mom was out of the bathroom, sitting on her bed holding a bottle of J&B Scotch close to her body and cradling it like a baby doll. She was clearly in the midst of a psychotic break, raving out of her mind, eyes wild and not focusing.

"You're trying to steal MMMMMMMYYYYY husband and children," Mom spat out, waving the bottle at me.

"What?" I asked, shocked. "What are you talking about?"

"Romola, your mother thinks you are trying to steal her husband and children," Mrs. Mendelson said in a very accusatory tone.

At that moment, I lost it. "Really?" I screamed at her. "Mrs. Mendelson, my father is in prison, and you see the state my mother is in." Then I faced my mother. "And Mom, what the hell do you want me to do? Let the kids run wild all over the place? Let them have parties with drugs, drinking and sex? I don't think so. Someone has to look out for them. Why don't you get out of bed and take care of them yourself? They're *your* children! And Dad's in jail, for God's sake. How the hell am I stealing him from you?" I was astonished.

This incident was bad enough, but then, just three days later, I came home from work to find that for some reason, Mom had searched my room and gone through the pocketbook I'd left at home. I was furious and went to her bedroom to confront her. Suddenly she grabbed a lamp from her bedside table, pulled out the extension cord, and came after me with it, as if to beat me. I was used to her threatening violence, so I warned her, "If you come near me with that, I will wrap it around your neck. You don't hit me, Mom, you talk to me like a normal human being!"

My attempt to placate her wasn't working. It never worked, and she lunged as if to thrash me, so I pulled the cord and she didn't let go. She fell to the floor holding on as I pulled her along the carpet, my adrenaline raging. She got up and started running after me. I ran downstairs, out the front door, and she followed in her goddamned nightgown. The kids were watching, terrified, and Risa called the police. Next thing I knew, a couple of officers were pulling up. I remember them being kind to me. They knew about my family.

The police questioned me as Mom ran back inside the house. I explained that Mom and I were having one of our unfortunate arguments. I tried to make light of it with the cops, but inside, I was shaking. *This is it*, I thought. *I cannot do this anymore. Like I learned at the START Center, I have to take care of me. The kids will be okay. We'll find a way...*

The very next day at work, on my lunch break, I walked to Macy's and rode the escalator up to a floor where there was an old-fashioned phone booth. I stepped into the booth and called Dad's lawyer, sobbing into the phone. "You've got to get my dad out of jail," I pleaded. "I can't handle this. Mom is so fucked up. She's either violent, or she's like a zombie, in bed all the time, doped up on pills, and I'm taking care of the three kids. Please! I can't take it anymore. I'm only 19—I can't do this by myself! Can't you please find a way to get my Dad out of jail? We need him here to help."

Chapter Seventeen

The King Returns to His Castle
1976-1978

After I made that desperate call from the phone booth upstairs at Macy's, the most extraordinary thing happened: Dad was granted early release from prison after serving eight months of a one-year sentence. While we were waiting for his paperwork to go through, things with Mom were still so horrible that I reached the point where I felt I couldn't take it anymore.

The next time Dad called us at home (he was allowed one call per week), I picked up the phone in the kitchen and sat at the desk crying. I told him about the incident with me and Mom and the police and said I needed to get away before something worse happened. I needed to start a life of my own and take care of myself. Dad had seen Mom and me go at it many times, and he was actually sympathetic this time, agreeing to help.

My friend Judy also had a very difficult mother, so Judy and I decided to move in together and share an apartment. I couldn't wait to start this new phase of my life, finally free and independent, on my own in the world and not constantly living in my father's shadow.

* * *

This decision to move out led to one of the most terrifying experiences of my life. I needed $2600 cash for the security deposit, first month's rent, and furniture for my new apartment, so Dad arranged for me to get the cash from his partner, Herb. I went to Dad's office on 42nd Street in the morning and picked up the cash from Herb. I left, but for some reason I can't recall now, I had to return to the office with the cash still in my wallet. There must have been something more I needed to talk about with Herb.

Anyway, it was raining hard that day, and as I walked, mud, dirt and water splashed onto the calves of my legs. Suddenly, two men—one tall and skinny, the other, large and heavy—approached me. The skinny guy gave me a lascivious look and said, "Hey, baby, can I help you get that dirt off your legs?"

"No, thanks," I replied and continued walking into the dark, dingy lobby of the building. As I entered the filthy, dilapidated elevator and stepped back into the corner, the larger man stuck his foot inside to block the elevator door from closing, then yelled to his buddy, "Hey, man, watch the front door!!" Then he stepped toward me, eyes blazing. "What's in your bag?" he asked me.

Are you kidding me? I thought. *Today of all days, someone wants to rob me?*

As he came toward me, I started to black out, my back sliding down the wall. (Boy, I certainly faint a lot, don't I?) I felt my body going limp as I was losing consciousness. Then, suddenly, I heard the skinny guy yell, "Hey, someone's coming!"

The larger man turned and bolted out of the elevator car just as the door pressed closed. My hands were shaking, my heart pounding, and I could barely breathe as I pushed the button for the fourth floor.

When the elevator door opened, I could hear the two men coming up the staircase, and when I looked across the hallway to Dad's office, I could see the door was closed and the lights were off. I ran out of the elevator and to the office, pulling on the door as hard as I could. It was locked!! My terror skyrocketed as I heard the men's voices coming closer. I looked at the stairs, desperately hoping someone was still in one of the offices up there. If I could make it up to the next level, I might be safe.

I ran up the stairs and, thank God, there was an office that was open. I ran in and started to cry, saying, "Two men are after me!" The guys from the office ran down the stairs and outside, but the would-be thieves were nowhere to be seen. I thanked the guys from the office again and again and then ran to Joey, who at the time was working for my dad in a store in a different building close by. Joey was so angry when I told him what happened, he grabbed a baseball bat to go after the bad guys. I told him they'd be long gone by now, but he didn't care.

At least I was safe. That was all I cared about. I couldn't bear to think what might have happened if that office on the fifth floor hadn't been open. To this day, I can't pass that building on 42nd Street without reliving that horrible experience, even though that run-down office building is long gone, replaced by a Chevys Fresh Mex. Some things just stay with you forever and are impossible to shake, no matter how hard you try.

* * *

When Dad was released from prison, they flew him from Florida back to New York, and Mom and I went to pick him up. He looked surprisingly good for having been locked up so long. He was thinner and more muscular, as he predicted in his letters, with a fresh haircut and a bit of a tan from being outside in the Florida sun. His thick, drooping, graying walrus mustache hadn't changed, though. He wouldn't be Marty without it.

I was surprised how glad I was to see him. He may have been my abuser, my tormentor, but he was also my father. It was unfortunate for me how fiercely I loved him.

On the way back home, Mom drove with Dad in the front passenger seat and me in back, just behind him. I mustered the courage to ask him the thing I'd wanted to ask him for so long. "Dad," I began carefully. "Why do you do the business you do? These past eight months have been so hard for all of us. Don't you see what this is doing to our family?"

Dad sighed. "Romola, I make $20,000 a week in my business. I can't give up that kind of money. I do what I do for my family. I do it for you. Your mother, brother, sisters and you."

Wow! Twenty grand a week?! That's more than a million dollars a year. I was shocked, and yet somehow understood how it would be really hard to walk away from that kind of money. I thought my Dad could do anything he set his mind to. He was smart. Maybe not highly educated, but street smart. I was so hopeful that when he got out of jail, he would be inspired to find a new livelihood. But now I could see why he wouldn't leave this huge empire behind. Dad had been hustling, working the streets since he was a kid, building businesses from the ground up, and making millions in the process.

Damn, I was glad he was home. That in itself was such a relief. *Now I can get away from Mom and from how awful life is with her.*

* * *

Judy and I got our apartment on the third floor of the Chesapeake House on 28th and Third, with windows in the bedroom and a living room that overlooked Third Avenue. Moving into the apartment made me feel frightened and excited at the same time. At age 19, no longer feeling the weight of responsibility of trying to care for my younger siblings, gave me some relief. I also felt very guilty about leaving them, but I tried to convince myself that Risa was old enough now and she'd be able to take over.

It didn't take me long to realize that it had been a mistake for Judy to come to New York with me. She wasn't ready to move out of her mother's home and ended up moving back there a few weeks later. Once again I found myself in a bad situation because there was no way I could afford the apartment on my own. So I put an ad in the classified section of the newspaper and got a series of really crazy roommates.

When the last one moved out (not a moment too soon), my friend Joni from school moved in. She is one of the most talented people I know, and she worked in the garment district making patterns for fabric. But then she, too, moved out and got her own place on the Upper East Side.

One night Joni and I went to Elaine's, the famous Upper East Side restaurant. Woody Allen was there and we were so drunk, we went over to him and told him how much we loved his work. He didn't seem pleased by our attention, and nor did Elaine. (Maybe, at age 19/20, we were already too old for Woody!)

That same night, Joni and I met four guys and took them home. I was in an experimental mood and was with three of them! They were really fun, adventurous guys, and we had a blast together! I think Joni was a bit surprised by my wildness—oops! Meanwhile, she stayed up talking to the fourth guy, if I remember correctly.

Those were some wild, wild times. We used to go to late-night dance clubs that were dark and sexy. We even went to the famous (or infamous) Studio 54 one night. As we were dancing, there was a tall, thin, black woman dancing, I could swear it was Grace Jones, twirling and twirling, and her short skirt would fly up around her hips, revealing that she wore no underwear. Alas, Joni soon left the Upper East Side to move downtown, and from there she moved to California with her husband-to-be, John.

I had the apartment on my own for a bit while I was working for the Reise brothers at "The Crowing Cock." Yeah, I know, great name, isn't it? It was actually a nice bar/restaurant in the middle of the garment district, 1375 Broadway. It turned out I was a terrible waitress, so they made me a hostess instead, and I loved it.

What heady days those were, in the mid-to-late '70s, when disco was king and Donna Summer was the queen. Those of us young enough to enjoy it would party nonstop. So many of the restaurant staff came to my apartment to party—old Italian men, gay guys, girls studying to be actresses—and we would bring home food and wine, put on Donna Summer records, and dance and party all night long. Many would sleep over, then we would all wake up in the morning and go to work!

At some point, I realized that I couldn't pay the bills all by myself, so Joey moved in, along with my friends Bob and Sue. Sue was a great waitress and Bob was unemployed at the time. The same time they moved in, a high-end prostitute, a madam, moved into the unit next to mine, and her bedroom and mine shared a common wall. That was crazy! I would hear all kinds of sexy stuff going on as I was trying to sleep. She even invited us to some of her parties, and boy, did we have fun!

Despite all the fun, we did try to focus somewhat on work. Joey took a position as an independent contractor with a messenger service using his van, and I started taking classes at Betty Owen Secretarial School, learning how to type. I also began having psychic experiences, just like my mother, which was very strange but also exciting.

One morning I went in to work and said to my coworker Maria, "Something bad is going to happen. Something terrible. I just know it." When I got home that evening, I still felt so upset. Sue was home and I was telling her how I just knew that something really bad was going to happen. Bob hadn't come home yet and neither had Joey. Of course there were no cell phones back then, so we had no way to call and check if they were okay.

By 11:00 p.m., both Sue and I were frantic. Suddenly Bob stumbled in, holding on to Joey, who was woozy and covered in blood and bandages. Apparently, the TR6 Joey was driving had gone under a tractor-trailer and people had to climb under the trailer to pull him out. Joey must have called Bob at the apartment to come pick him up. Joey was hurt and shaken up, but he would be okay.

I was shocked to think that I had had this premonition of something terrible happening all day, the fear and dread growing stronger by the hour, and then it came true. *Am I like my mother?* I thought with glee. Imagine having some kind of power that allows you to know when something good or bad will happen. To some people, being happy about that might sound weird, but to me, it was amazing. In fact, I was later able to focus this energy into my healing work, which I'll describe later.

* * *

Fortunately, we had more fun moments than supernatural. Bob and Sue had a lovely white Lab named Liberty and I had a horrible cat named Sugar, and both ended up pregnant at the same time. Liberty gave birth to eight puppies. Two days later, Joey and I were sleeping on the pull-out couch in the living room when I felt something wet. Sugar had started giving birth in bed with us! Then, while still in labor, she picked herself up with the kitten half-delivered and moved into the closet, where she gave birth to a litter of four kittens. What joy this was! Every night after that, the four of us humans would place the four kittens and eight puppies on the living room floor and play with them, rolling around and giggling. It broke our hearts to get rid of them, but eventually, Sue found each of them a good home.

Looking back, I'm so glad I spent part of my young adulthood living with Joey, Bob and Sue, just working, dancing, partying, and having fun. Some of my best memories are of all The Grateful Dead concerts the four of us attended. (I still love the Grateful Dead to this day!) It was such a relief, and a release, from my crazy, violent, unpredictable childhood. I had been so scared, sad, and angry for so many years that feeling this way became my default, my norm. I had no idea what normal life was like, or how to be young, carefree and happy like my peers. But living at The Chesapeake gave me some of that back, allowing me to experience so much of what I had missed.

* * *

On May 17th, 1978, my life changed forever. Francesca's was a fancy French restaurant, very chic and expensive, a place we only went for special occasions. When Joey took me there that Wednesday evening, I was shocked. *Why are we here? And on a Wednesday? It's so expensive...*

Joey seemed uncharacteristically nervous that warm spring night as we walked down the three steps into the cute little restaurant. The hostess led us to our table and Joey pulled out my chair. As I sat, he got down on one knee, pulled out a little square box, opened it to reveal a ring, and said, voice shaking, "Romola, will you marry me?"

I was shocked, but immediately said yes. I was 20, just three weeks away from turning 21, and the timing felt right. Even if I had some deep-down doubts, that was normal, right? I loved Joey and he loved me, and that was all that mattered. Or so I hoped.

We spent five days celebrating our engagement. On the fourth day, we told Joey's family during dinner at Beef Steak Charlie's. They all seemed happy for us. On the fifth day, we took my parents out to an expensive steakhouse in Cedarhurst called Werner Baer's. Dad ordered the steak tartare. I remember this so vividly, because when Joey and I announced that we were engaged, Dad's food had just arrived, and he was so shocked, he didn't eat any of his steak. I tried really hard not to notice; I so wanted him to be happy for us. His approval still meant the world to me.

Jarrett was probably the most excited of anyone; he loved Joey and looked up to him like an older brother. Mom and Rhonda also seemed really happy. Risa at first seemed subdued, but then embraced the idea. I suspect that deep down, she, like Dad, also thought that Joey and I were not right for each other.

What the hell is wrong with me? I thought. Here I was, on what was supposed to be one of the happiest nights of my life. It was wonderful, and yet I couldn't get the image of Dad's unhappy face out of my mind. He was trying to be happy for us, I could see that, but his pasted-on smile looked hollow, false. I kept hearkening back to that conversation we'd had when I was home from the START Center with my broken ankle, and he'd said, "You and Joey are so different. You are so much deeper, so much more complex than he is. I just don't think he's right for you."

Maybe Dad, too, was remembering that conversation, and that was why he looked so sad and disappointed. *Am I getting married for the right reasons?* I had to ask myself. *I love Joey, but does a part of me see marrying him as an attempt to prove Dad wrong?*

Chapter Eighteen

The Princess Becomes a Bride, But Finds True Love with Another
1978-1982

Whatever doubts I might have had about my engagement to Joey, I threw myself wholeheartedly into planning the wedding and preparing for our life together as husband and wife. During this time, Joey started working for my Dad again, collecting money or working behind the counter at one of Dad's 42nd Street stores. I didn't like it when Joey started bringing home porno tapes and wanted to watch them with me. I'm no prude, but the movies were so strange and silly, they just never turned me on.

Dad was pressuring Joey and me to move to Pensacola, Florida, where, since getting out of prison, Dad was expanding his porn empire through adult book and video stores. He offered Joey the chance to manage six stores down there, which would mean making a lot of money, but I said no. I had spent my whole childhood trying to extricate myself from Dad's grasp, and from my identity as the daughter of the King of Porn.

Joey working for Dad was one thing, he could quit anytime, but managing stores was another. If we did that, Joey and I would never have an independent life of our own; we would always be living under Dad's thumb. I realized later that I should have let Joey go to school to become a forest ranger, which is what he really wanted to do. I just couldn't see myself living in a forest somewhere, wearing lots of plaid flannel and worrying about bears. I still feel badly, though, that I may have kept Joey from living his dream.

* * *

Things started to change in the spring of 1979 when the lease on our apartment at the Chesapeake was up. Bob and Sue were heading to Florida and Joey and I found a place in Kew Gardens in Queens. The parting was bittersweet—one Sunday, the four of us had a Jack Daniel's party and we each wrote on a piece of paper our feelings for each other. I still treasure this keepsake in my scrapbook to this day.

* * *

We had been engaged for almost a year and a half when Joey and I got married on Saturday, October 6, 1979. What a wedding! What a party! We had a priest and a rabbi, along with both our families, our friends and many of Dad's crazy colleagues and associates. My bridesmaids were Risa, Rhonda, Sue and Liz, while Joey's attendants were his brothers, Scott and Craig, along with our friend Bob.

The exquisite $80,000 ceremony was held at Terrace on the Park in Queens, an extraordinary venue set on the former grounds of the New York World's Fair, in what had been the fair's heliport, situated high above Flushing Meadow Park. The panoramic views of the New York City skyline were breathtaking, and the whole venue seemed to be suspended in midair. It was a magical location for a magical day. Everyone was so happy, but especially Dad. In the Jewish tradition, he sat on a chair and was hoisted high in the air, danced around the room and celebrated by those who held him up.

There was one special moment that I will treasure forever. Dad walked me down the aisle to the melody of "The Wedding March," and when we reached the altar, just before he left me beside Joey, he squeezed my hand. Just briefly, wordlessly, and then he went to sit with Mom in the front row. My dad was never one for showing affection, so I think this was his way of expressing his love and giving his blessing to my union with Joey. That meant so much to me, especially since I knew he hadn't been thrilled about the engagement.

The live music was great, and both drugs and drink were consumed in vast quantities. At one point, when the celebration was in high gear, I took a step back and just looked at everything, drinking it all in—the wedding cake, the live band, the white tablecloths, the gorgeous decorations and thought, *Am I really doing the right thing?* Somehow, I just knew I had to marry Joey and hope that it worked out.

The Princess of 42nd Street

* * *

Joey and I honeymooned in Freeport, but by the time we came home, our relationship was already showing some cracks. We moved to Bayside in Queens and Joey was partying a lot. We had both started working for a company that involved us taking Joey's van and traveling around America setting up art auctions. We could earn up to $1,000 a week, which sounds like a lot for the time, but when we figured in the cost of gasoline, parking, food, lodging, etc., it just didn't make sense financially for me to keep traveling with Joey, so I didn't. So now we were spending a lot of time apart, which wasn't great for our marriage, and when we were together, things weren't perfect, either.

Now that we were married, I was hoping to settle down, but Joey preferred to continue partying, and that created a lot of friction. Back in the '70s, partying was a regular part of life, but Joey's partying was really affecting me. One day I came home to find Joey passed out, the dinner burnt, and an LP record skipping on the turntable. I couldn't take it anymore, so only six months into our marriage, I made the difficult decision to leave him.

A few months before I got married, my friend Liz married her boyfriend, Arthur, but they split up very quickly. Now Liz was living in a friend's apartment on 78th Street, between First and Second Avenue in Manhattan, so I went to stay with her while I was figuring out if I wanted to work things out with Joey or if it would be better to make our separation permanent.

Liz's apartment was exciting but horrible; the first night I slept there, I woke up with two cockroaches crawling all over me. This was a sixth-floor walk-up and that's how it was back then. Living conditions aside, I felt like a huge weight had been lifted from me, like I was on a vacation from my life. But I was also drinking more than I should, and I started hanging out at a bar on Second Avenue and 78th Street. I would walk into the bar and scan it for any good-looking guys to take back to the apartment. Most of the time it was fun, but then one night, not so much. I was at the bar and I didn't see anyone who interested me, so after a few drinks, I picked up the only guy who looked somewhat reasonable and brought him back to the walk-up.

When I woke up early the next morning and glanced over at this person sleeping beside me, I felt sick. He was so unattractive, and at that moment I realized I had a problem. I woke him up and asked him to leave as gently as I could. Later, I sat with Liz and talked with her about how this bad habit had to stop. "This isn't really me,' I told her. "This isn't the way I want to live my life."

Soon after, Liz introduced me to a guy named Michael whom I really liked. We hung out together for a week. He was a Vietnam vet who smoked too much pot, but he was so good looking. I had no idea where this relationship might go, but in the end, I didn't have time to find out. I got a phone call from Joey, telling me he needed to have an operation. It was something to do with all the driving he was doing and a vein wrapped around one of his testicles. He was in a lot of pain, and said he missed me so much and wanted me home. So, against my better judgment, I went back to him. I felt like he needed me, and maybe I felt it was my duty as a wife to be by his side.

I knew within days that going back was a mistake, but I stayed anyway. I had such a history with him; I had been with him since I was 13. He was always my safe port in the storm when things got rough. But with all we had been through, I had lost some respect for him, and that was the real issue. I realized how important it is to not only love someone but also to respect the person you're with. I knew I should leave, but on some level, I was staying with Joey because I couldn't bear hearing Dad say, "I told you so." How sad this was, both for me and for Joey. We stayed in the same place, unable to move forward.

* * *

In 1982, Risa married her boyfriend, Alex. Risa met Alex at a school where they were both learning how to make false teeth. Alex always came to class with such unhealthy sandwiches his father had made for him, bread layered thick with butter and one tiny piece of meat. Risa felt sorry for him, so she made him big, thick sandwiches and gave them to him in class.

Alex and his family came from Ukraine, and his mom had died from complications of diabetes when he was 18. He was a wild kid, really good looking, and Risa fell hard. I remember going to his dad's

The Princess of 42nd Street

apartment and his dad, Izzy, bringing in a tray with vodka in little shot glasses. I loved Izzy right from the beginning.

When Joey and I were on the way to Risa and Alex's wedding in the van, we were running late and Joey was high on Quaaludes, so he probably shouldn't have been driving. Suddenly, a vehicle slammed into us at full speed and the van overturned with us inside. I opened my eyes, saw pink fluid everywhere, and started screaming that it was blood. It was actually only transmission fluid, but I was in shock and confused. It felt like I was in a dream as a man reached in and helped pull me out from under the van.

Joey and I were both hurt, not to mention very shaken up, but nothing was going to keep me from seeing my little sister get married. Amazingly, we made it to the wedding, even though Joey and I were both in a lot of pain. While at the wedding, someone gave me a Valium, and that really helped me relax.

The wedding was beautiful, even though I got through most of it in a fog of pain and confusion caused by the accident and the Valium. I found out years later that the wedding was where my dad met his future "lovely" wife Andrea. Mom and Dad were still married at this point; they would divorce in 1989 and Dad married Andrea in 2000. Andrea was dating one of Dad's friends, but Dad must have been wealthier than his friend, because Andrea seemed determined to marry the man with the most money.

After the car accident, I continued having a lot of chronic pain and discomfort, especially in my lower back and shoulders. Doctors didn't seem to have the answer, so I started seeing a physical therapist named Carlos twice a week. Carlos would change my life, not just physically, but emotionally and spiritually as well. I was working as a secretary at a law firm at the time, and Carlos showed me a world beyond anything I had imagined, turning me on to aromatherapy, Swedish massage, meditation, essential oils, New Age philosophy and the mind/body connection.

Carlos also demonstrated amazing insight when I talked to him about my mother. He explained about her back issues, and how the chronic pain she had in her back was related to the psychological issues that had plagued her all her life. He helped me see my mother in a kinder, more generous light.

I fell for Carlos completely. He was so kind and real. He cared about the environment and became a vegetarian long before it was so popular. Of course it didn't hurt that he was great looking. Puerto Rican with a round face, dazzling smile, jet-black hair and a deep skin tone, he was handsome, Latin, sensitive and sensual. He told me he was in the process of starting his own business, and I admired his ambition and drive.

Joey was still traveling a lot during this period, setting up the art auctions, so I spent a lot of time home alone. And even when Joey was there, he was high much of the time and not at all attentive. It was clear to me that our marriage was not going to last, but I had no idea how to end it. The thought alone was heartbreaking.

* * *

I had been seeing Carlos for physical therapy twice a week for two months when something changed. During one of our sessions, I was lying on the table, relaxing with a heat pack. Slowly, my eyes drifted open and there was Carlos, staring right at me. *Holy shit! I mean, holy shit. What is happening to me?* We couldn't stop staring into each other's eyes. Finally, he said, "Will you wait for me after work?"

I thought for a moment. "Yes," I answered breathlessly. Normally, after my hour-long visit with Carlos, I would spend an hour in Greenwich Village before taking the train home. I loved to sit in Washington Park Square and listen to the people playing music and dancing, selling all sorts of trinkets and things. But this day, I didn't go home after the Village; I returned to Carlos's office on 14th Street between Eighth and Ninth Avenue. I was so nervous as I waited. *Do I look okay? How's my hair? What the fuck am I doing here, anyway? I should just go home.* But then Carlos emerged from the building and gave me a big smile, putting all my fears at ease.

We went to a bar in Greenwich Village that was famous for having 280 different kinds of beer. I never much cared for beer, but I did care for Carlos. We had a few drinks and then he kissed me. And what a kiss! So passionate and sensual, like nothing I had ever experienced before.

From the bar we went to Carlos' apartment on Jane Street off Bleecker in the Village, where we continued kissing, going further and further. Then we made our way to the mattress he had on the floor. He was so gentle, yet also so confident and assured, I just let my body submit to his touch. Slowly, surely, he began removing my clothes, one item at a time, my heart pounding, until I was down to my underwear. Then, he started rubbing jasmine essential oil all over my body, warming me with his strong hands, before he sprinkled red rose petals all across my body, letting them drift slowly onto my skin and into my hair.

He was such a skilled and expert lover; only after he had me nice and warm and relaxed did he undress himself. And I was in for a freakin' shock! When Carlos took off his underpants and I saw the enormous size of his maleness, I screamed, jumped off the mattress, and ran to hide behind a chair, just like a scene in a movie. "You are NOT putting that thing inside of me," I insisted. "It is HUGE!! You'll kill me!"

He laughed. "Don't worry, I won't hurt you," he promised as he came closer and took my hand, leading me back toward the mattress. And then he made the softest, slowest, most deliciously sensual love to me. It was so easy, and so wonderful.

Soon, Carlos and I couldn't get enough of each other, and I found myself counting the minutes until I could see him again. I had incredibly deep and powerful feelings for him. I told him I was planning to leave Joey—not because of him, I'd been planning to leave for a while—but asked if he would be there for me. He promised he would.

Soon, we were deeply in love. We would walk down the street and just stop in the middle of a crowd of people and start making out. As I rode the bus down Seventh Avenue on my way to see him, the anticipation was intense and delicious. I couldn't wait to lose myself in his embrace. I would jump off the bus, then sprint down the street to his apartment off Bleecker. I knocked on the door and when he opened it, I just jumped into his arms.

At some point, Joey must have had suspicions because he went into my pocketbook and found a love letter Carlos had written me. He was furious and no doubt very hurt. When I got home, he started screaming that he was going to go to Carlos's office to beat him up. I was so nervous at work the next day, I couldn't concentrate, afraid of what might happen if Joey and Carlos went at it.

Fortunately, when Joey got to Carlos's office, the staff would not let him in. I felt embarrassed and feared Carlos would wonder what the hell he had gotten himself into with me. I was so unfocused and making so many mistakes in my job at the law office, I finally had to tell my employers what was going on in my life. As much as they sympathized, they had to let me go because of all the typos I made and then failed to catch.

Violence between Joey and Carlos was averted, but I knew we couldn't go on like this forever. I finally told Joey that I was leaving him. He was devastated, as was his mother, who told me I needed to go back and take care of him. *No, not this time*, I thought. *This is the best decision for both Joey and me.* At least Dad didn't gloat about it; if he was feeling "I told you so," he kept those thoughts to himself.

After Joey and I divorced, he wound up dating an older woman for a while and then married a friend of mine from college. That marriage didn't last long, but they did have a beautiful baby daughter. He and I are still in touch today and are on good terms.

* * *

Life with Carlos was everything I hoped it would be—thrilling, engaging and inspiring, not to mention full of fantastic sex! We hadn't been together long when there was a fire and his apartment burned down. We ended up moving in with his mother in the housing projects on Houston and FDR Drive. Carlos' mother loved me, and I loved her in return, even if there were some awkward moments at first. The apartment was so small, and the walls were very thin. When Carlos and I made love, it was so orgasmic that I would scream with pleasure. But then I felt so embarrassed the next morning, not wanting to face his mom, knowing everything she must have heard the night before.

But to my pleasure and surprise, she greeted me the next morning with a broad smile on her face. "Come now, have some breakfast," she said, sitting me down at the table. I imagine she was happy that her son was with a woman who truly loved and appreciated him. But still, inside, I was really embarrassed.

Carlos' mom was a fantastic cook. My favorite dish was her rice and beans, which she cooked in a traditional method with olive oil.

The Princess of 42nd Street

The oil makes the rice brown and crunchy and stick to the bottom of the pan and you have to peel it up to eat it. This is the most delicious part of the dish, and Carlos and his mom always gave it to me. Why is it that people who have the least often give you the most?

The dish also included a delicious herb whose flavor I didn't recognize, and neither of them knew the name in English. Years later I found out it was cilantro, and now I cook with it all the time. I've tried making the rice and beans myself and I just can't get it right. A secret family recipe, I suppose!

For a girl who'd grown up in the Five Towns on Long Island, the housing projects were like another world, rife with crime and drugs and elevators that were always broken down and smelled like urine. In my naivety, I had never understood why people who were poor lived with such dirt and squalor, but now I understood. I saw the hell that people went through who were poor and oppressed, and I witnessed firsthand the anger, hurt and despair it causes. Soon Carlos got an apartment on 86th and Columbus. This is where I started my first business, Health's Happening. I did nutritional consultation, massage and energy work.

Meeting and moving in with Carlos became a major turning point in my life. He helped me finally discover what I was good at and what I wanted to dedicate my life to—learning, helping and healing. Carlos opened my mind and heart to so many new things, and he taught me about massage and being a vegetarian. Inspired by him, I found my passion to build a career as a healer. I wanted to be good to myself and help educate others to do the same.

Over time I would complete Gary Null's holistic counseling certificate course, and then attend the Lawrence Harrison Institute to further my knowledge of nutrition and energy healing modalities. I also became certified as a Laura Norman reflexologist, studying with Ms. Norman herself! I also studied polarity, shiatsu and the Trager Approach. Years later, I would go into the health field, the natural food industry in particular, and become one of the first women to own my own business as a broker, a business I ran successfully for 22 years.

But all that would come later. As I sat on a bench outside Carlos' mom's apartment in the projects, looking out over the decaying urban wasteland with its burnt-out cars, broken pavement and people hanging out on street corners dancing and drinking, I felt a million miles away from the luxury of 37 Harborview West, from the gaudy lights of Times Square, from the porn shops and peep show machines of 42nd Street. "That's Dad's world," I thought. "The universe of Martin Hodas. It has nothing to do with me. I'll always be my father's daughter, the firstborn child of New York's King of Porn, but that's an identity, not a life sentence. I am my own woman, and I have found myself at last."

Chapter Nineteen

The King of Porn Passes On
2014

May 24th, 2014: I was at Risa's when her home phone buzzed. She was away, visiting her daughters, Leyna and Veronica, in Chicago, and I had been living at her place in Bayside, Queens ever since my life took a horrible turn in 2009. I looked down, recognizing the number as my sister Rhonda's, and steeled myself to hear the news I knew was coming but that no one can ever really be prepared for.

"Hello?" I said, swallowing hard, my heart pounding in my throat.

"Romola, Daddy died," Rhonda whispered in a soft, low voice. I could tell she had been crying. In the moments before the wave of my own grief washed over me, I wished so much that I could comfort Rhonda, but we have such a difficult relationship. This wasn't going to be easy for any of us, but it would be so much easier if we had each other to lean on and support.

Daddy died. Even though you know it's coming, it sounds completely surreal when you finally hear those words. "Daddy died." I said it out loud to see how it sounded, to see how the words felt on my lips, but even that didn't make it real.

I was sitting in Risa's bed watching TV, alone. The entire family had been waiting for this call; we had known for a while that it was just a matter of time. But still, I could not picture a world that no longer included Marty Hodas in it; Dad was so much a part of my life, my identity, my reality, that I couldn't imagine a future without him. *And now he is gone. I'll never see Dad again.* The words shook me to my very core. I was almost 57 years old, and suddenly I felt like an orphan. *I'm alone now. I don't have parents anymore.*

After hanging up with Rhonda, I wept until all my tears were gone. Then I pulled myself together and phoned Andrea to ask how it happened. Talking to her was not going to be easy for me, but I put that aside. When we spoke, she claimed that Dad had gone into the bathroom, came out, collapsed on the bed, and stopped breathing. I was immediately suspicious. Just two days before his death, Dad had had a talk with Rhonda and her husband, Alan. We all believed that Dad intended to make Alan the executor of his will but that Andrea had pressured him into keeping her in charge of everything instead.

I believe Alan and Rhonda helped Dad see that we would all be screwed if Andrea were in control of the estate. We also wondered if the stress of fighting with Andrea about the will was really what triggered Dad's death, especially considering that his health was already in a highly precarious state at that point.

We all felt that Andrea disliked us, but Dad didn't seem to want to believe the wife he loved could be so cruel to his children. Andrea didn't even try to hide her contempt for us. My parents ended up divorcing in 1989, when I was 37, and Dad married Andrea in 2000. (As I mentioned, they first met at Risa's wedding in 1982.)

After Mom passed away, Dad told Jarrett to go and get all of Mom's jewelry, which he did. We, the three sisters, understood why Jarrett did this. He worked for our father, and Dad could be so mean and scary. He just wouldn't take no for an answer. Jarrett has felt guilty about this for years, but I wish he didn't, because we understand.

Once Dad had Mom's jewelry, Andrea had no qualms about helping herself to some of the pieces, especially those that had real jewels. Many of the rings were not real diamonds, and those she didn't mind letting us have. The $30,000 watch is gone. We all hoped that eventually, we would get back our mother's jewelry, along with photos and whatever else was rightfully ours.

When we told Andrea we wanted the jewelry back, she said that our mother's will stated that our dad would get all her jewelry when she passed away. Huh? Mom bequeathed her jewelry to the ex-husband she despised? I don't think so!

Jarrett had a copy of Mom's will and of course there was no mention of Marty getting all Mom's jewelry upon her death. Andrea had also taken some of the pictures my mother had in the living room that Dad took for his office. I was hoping to get them back but she would never have that conversation with us. There were things that could mean nothing to Andrea but that meant everything to us—even all of Dad's *tchotchke* that she hated. I hoped she would give them to us, but all we got was a box full of broken, damaged and dusty irrelevant things. I was heartbroken—we all were.

Mom's later years were desperately sad before she died in 2004 at 66 with her mind completely gone. Her bipolar and personality disorder continued to plague her, and she was agoraphobic for 30 years. She became addicted to QVC and spent tons of money on jewelry and things she couldn't afford. Then she moved to Florida to be near Jarrett because she had spent so much of her money and had to give up the house that I always thought would be mine.

I was really worried about the toll that moving would take on her, and unfortunately, my fears were not unfounded because a month into the move, she suffered a heart attack and stroke simultaneously and was in terrible shape. Jarrett and his wife, Toi, took care of her as best they could, but she ended up having her foot amputated due to complications of diabetes, and she died in a nursing home that March.

Once Dad knew he was dying, he tried to reassure us. "Don't worry; by the time I've been gone three weeks, you will all be fine." He firmly believed that Andrea would take care of Jarrett financially until all the estate details had been worked out. Dad was always good at not seeing the things he didn't want to see. (A few years before Dad's death, Jarrett had a gun accident, which blinded him and destroyed his ability to speak, and also caused other severe, life-altering injuries.)

But sorting out that financial mess would all come later. I brought my attention back to the present. I dreaded what I had to do next—call Risa and tell her the terrible news. I knew she'd be devastated. Since Risa's husband, Alex, had worked for Dad, Risa had become somewhat closer to him. She even tried to get closer to Andrea, but Andrea hated Dad giving his children any attention or money.

Risa only lived five minutes away from them and they all used to go out to dinner and the movies quite often. I think Risa enjoyed their company. Alex had passed away—another death from complications of diabetes—her daughters were grown up and out of the house, and she lived alone, except for her dog and cat and now me. I'd been living with her since I left the city following my third divorce and the loss of my business in the natural food industry, which I'd had for 22 years. (Carlos was wonderful, but things with us didn't work out long term; I ended up marrying and divorcing two more times after Joey.) For so long I'd been feeling like a bomb had exploded in the middle of my world, and on top of that, I felt so alone. I wanted Risa here with me; I wanted somebody. I wanted my dogs. I shared them with my ex and he had them that week.

I phoned Risa and she took the news about Dad hard, as I expected. Even though we all knew Dad was dying, none of us were ready to accept it, and the rawness of Risa's pain was like a punch in my gut. We cried together for a while, and after we hung up, I cried even longer on my own, curled up in Risa's bed and missing her, missing Dad, missing every good thing my life had been, feeling nothing but pain and loss and stomach-churning grief.

After a while, I sat up, squared my shoulders, and reminded myself of something that has been so important throughout my life: I had stayed sane and survived everything I had survived because of my attitude. My attitude is what will make or break me. I choose courage. *And that's exactly how I will handle Dad's death*, I told myself. I grabbed my laptop and started listening to some Esther Hicks, then looked up meditations for courage and letting go of grief. I needed to make myself as strong as possible to handle whatever lay ahead.

Thank God I had become a leader in the moderation management movement, designed to help problem drinkers learn to drink responsibly, otherwise I would have turned to alcohol to drown my sorrows at this terrible moment, and my drinking would be off the charts! I certainly did drink more than I wanted to, but always had in my head to do the best I could. This time would pass and I would get it under control again.

Dad was 82 years old when he died, and the official cause of death was COPD, chronic obstructive pulmonary disease, and chronic obstructive airway disease, among other health issues. While he was ill, I had tried to help him as best I could. Even though our relationship never stopped being contentious over the decades, my love for him never wavered. Complicated, but always present.

While his health was declining, Dad had been surprisingly open to trying the new alternative health treatments I suggested, informed by my 25 years as a leader in the natural health industry, but Andrea was hostile and negative, constantly telling him, "Herbs are ridiculous." She ridiculed and dismissed anything that my siblings or I tried to do for Dad. I had done all I could for him, and he had even tried a new type of stem-cell therapy in hopes of getting better, but nothing really seemed to work.

Days before Dad died, he and Andrea had returned from spending six months in Florida. I worried about how he would do on the airplane coming back to New York in his condition. He was not in good shape and I wished he would have stayed in Florida longer to recover. But Dad and Andrea were snowbirds and it was the trendy time to come home; never mind him being ill, Andrea seemed to have plans.

Risa had been planning to go to Chicago to see her daughters, but I had a feeling that we should go see Dad before she went to Chicago. Call it intuition, a second sense, whatever, a feeling of deep urgency told me we needed to do this, and we needed to do it now.

When I phoned Dad to ask about Risa and me coming to visit, we were told that all had gone well on the flight home, which we later found out wasn't true. Dad had been quite ill and even fainted on the plane.

"Let's go say hello to Dad before you leave for Chicago," I suggested to Risa. A part of me suspected that he didn't have long. And a psychic, my feng shui teacher, Barry, had just recently told me that he believed my dad would be gone very soon. Looking back, I am so glad we decided to visit!

"That's a good idea," Risa agreed. Like all of us, her issues with Dad had affected her for her entire life. For a while she did secretarial work for Dad in his office and they had become very close, even though he never stopped torturing her with horrible names, calling her stupid and making fun of her ears. And seeing how he had tormented me about my weight all my life really affected her, too.

So, Risa and I made a visit to Dad. They were living in the North Shore Towers in New Hyde Park, a gated, luxury condo and country club community located on the Nassau County border between New York and Queens. Their residence was a luxurious high-rise with spectacular views including an 18-hole golf course, tennis courts and outdoor pools. In the winter, they lived in wealthy Turnberry Isle in Florida, another home to the rich.

One amazing trait about my dad—he always landed on his feet financially, no matter what happened to him, personally or professionally, or what setbacks he faced. After his conviction and prison term for tax evasion in 1975, he would never again hold the title of New York's undisputed "King of Porn." The introduction and widespread adoption of the VHS tape in the late 1970s, along with the rise of cable and pay-per-view television saw to that, making it much easier for people to access and enjoy pornography in the privacy of their own homes, without having to risk exposure and humiliation by attending a live sex act or going to a peep show. In response, Dad sold many of his Times Square businesses and properties and explored new business ventures. He was often successful, but he never made as much money, or as quickly, as he did with porn.

In 1984, Dad was the target of an undercover sting operation, "Operation Blizzard," that accused him of trying to transport 1700 porn videos over the border and into Canada. He was arrested and charged with conspiring to ship obscene material across state lines. He pled guilty and once again spent a year in prison, this time at a federal penitentiary in Lewisburg, Pennsylvania. After his release, he sold his remaining Times Square properties to a competitor for a fraction of their value.

When he was in jail, Mom finally found the courage to divorce him. He was shocked and devastated; I don't think he believed she would ever actually go through with it. I don't think any of us did.

It was so hard for me when he came home from jail this time. He again rented a home in Atlantic Beach and he was a wreck when I went to see him. He loved Mom like crazy, we all knew this, even though he abused her and treated her so badly.

Still, even after a second jail term, Marty Hodas may have been down, but he was not out. Out of New York, maybe, but not out of the porn business. He grew a new business, a huge adult bookstore in Miami, and by 1994, he had returned to Times Square, if not as the King of Porn, then at least a crown prince as he purchased several porn palaces including the Playpen, Playworld, and Peeporama, which he kind of stole from my brother-in-law Alex (I'll explain later). Apparently, there was still some market for onsite porn, even given the competition from video rentals and cable and pay-per-view TV.

Later things would get very complicated for the family, business-wise. While Dad was in jail, Alex started to partner with some of Dad's competition, and after Dad got out, he weaseled his

The Princess of 42nd Street

way in on that. That was the beginning of hell for Alex. Jarrett was working for Dad then, in Miami, as was Alex, in New York. They both tried to get him to create websites for the businesses and to start marketing online, but Dad didn't see the future in that (a rare misstep for him, business-wise), and we all believe his career suffered from his inability to evolve with the times.

Poor Alex. He really looked up to my dad and Dad wound up crushing him. While Dad was in prison, Alex went into business with Dad's ex-partner John. You know, the one the cops said was actually John "Sonny" Franzese, member of the Colombo crime family, when they found that note in Dad's desk during a raid on his office in 1972.

Anyway, the "real" John had lots of stores and he and Alex partnered in the three I mentioned, Playworld, Playpen, and Peeporama. Somehow my dad took the stores out from under Alex. There was some business stuff going on after a while and Dad pressured Alex to go to court and lie for him about Alex's ex-partners. Alex was shocked and didn't know what to do.

Soon after, something happened with the Russian mob. Some girls started working in the porn shops and we found out that these girls were teens trafficked from Russia. The police said that Alex was in on it, and Dad refused to help with a lawyer.

Thank God, Alex didn't need a lawyer because it was clear he had nothing to do with the Russian girls. But all this and a few other things really took a toll on Alex. He had a breakdown and left the business. He ended up selling drugs to make a living and it was heartbreaking.

Alex's downward spiral continued. Next thing we knew, he was arrested for being in a car with a woman who was driving, swerving the car because she was on drugs, and he had a loaded gun. He was sentenced to two years in prison and served 18 months.

Risa and he had been estranged for a few years by then, but she and I took him to jail. It was horrible. When he got out, he lived in a halfway house ten minutes from my cottage on Long Island. I would invite him over, so he could cook and help me with stuff. I wanted him to feel loved and needed.

One day Alex came over and I noticed something on his leg. "What's wrong with your leg?" I asked, concerned.

He looked down and shrugged. "It's nothing," he replied.

"No, Alex, something is really wrong. Let me take a look." So I went over and looked at his foot and leg, and what I saw shocked and horrified me. He had stepped on a nail that had gone through the sole of his boot and up into his foot, but because of his diabetes, he didn't feel a thing. On his calf was a long, red, horrible line. I knew this was a serious infection. I took him to the hospital immediately. Months later he had to have his foot amputated, then died of a heart attack aged only 56. Crazy man, but I miss him.

Both Risa and I were devastated by the loss of this creative, tortured soul. I think it hit me harder than it hit her because they had been estranged so long. We had to go tell Alex's father, Izzy, that his son had died, and also tell Leyna and Veronica that their father was gone. Those were some of the hardest moments of my life. Alex was cremated, and his ashes are still with Izzy, at his home.

* * *

As I got older, I became so involved in my own life and career that I didn't keep as many tabs on what Dad was doing, businesswise. I did know that he partnered with Sharon's Sorbet, and also got involved with Cobroxin, a cobra venom designed to treat arthritis pain, and later worked on lending money for second mortgages. But he never completely left porn behind. Porn was his baby, always calling him back home. In fact, he owned the Miami Playground until a year or two before he died. Dad never stopped hustling, never stopped looking for ways to earn a buck, and Martin Hodas, who grew up shining shoes and hawking newspapers, died a wealthy man.

* * *

When Risa and I first arrived at Dad's for our visit, I felt nervous, unsure of what we'd find. We knocked, and it took Dad several minutes to get to the door before he opened it. The image I saw took my breath away, and I had to stop myself from gasping. Dressed in baggy sweatpants and a T-shirt, he dragged his oxygen machine beside him with the breathing tube clipped into his nose. He was huffing and sweating, totally out of breath, just from those few steps. I was so shocked, hurt, and dismayed by seeing Dad reduced to this, and Risa clearly felt the same. I was so glad we had each other here for support.

Dad's skin hung loose around his cheeks and jowls, with wrinkly folds down his arms, like a really old man. *Shit*, I thought, drawing a sharp breath, *this man is not my father*. He had lost so much muscle. Even though he still had his signature stocky build, all his muscle tone was gone. I was scared shitless. I didn't want to admit what I knew in my heart that the end was near. I had read an article about an adult child seeing the change in her parents, watching them grow old from illness, but still, seeing this with my own eyes freaked me out.

Andrea wasn't home, which was fine with Risa and me. Andrea did not like us coming to visit, even though for many years her two daughters would come on Tuesdays. It was so hard for me to just let that go. But I knew it would eat me up inside if I didn't learn to be at peace with it. I tried to get along with Andrea's daughters, but Andrea seemed determined that we would all wind up disliking each other. This is so very sad, because I actually really liked them.

"C'mon in," Daddy said, opening the door wide. His face was pale and haggard, with a tired, worn-out expression. *God, he looks so old.* The once rambunctious, "life of the party" was wasting away. I'm not sure I truly realized how much I loved him until that moment. When I was younger and he would accuse me so many times of wanting him only for his money, I would always reply, "I wish that were true; my life would be a lot easier!"

It was only about 30 steps from the front door to Dad's office. I shot Risa a look that said, *"Oh my God!"* He was in pitiful shape. After shuffling along and taking those 30 steps to his office, Dad collapsed into his chair. He struggled for five minutes before he could speak, trying to catch his breath. I could feel myself starting to cry, but I forced back the tears.

"Daddy, are you doing all right?" I asked carefully.

"I'm good, as good as I'll ever be," he replied. He managed a half-smile, but I knew he wasn't fine. He was hunched over for a while, then started to sit up.

"Can I get you some water or anything?" Risa asked softly.

"I'm fine."

Then he relaxed and, when his breathing was easier, unbelievably, he started telling us stories, stories I always wanted to know. *Why now?* I wondered. These were things I knew had happened but Mom held them back from us. Now, he was free to reveal everything. Death does that sometimes, opens the floodgates that were shut tight for so long.

He started by telling us about when he was in jail. They were stories about his alliance with the Irish mob, stories about some of the other prisoners. Risa and I giggled at a few of the stories and grimaced at others. His energy seemed to perk up as he became the center of attention yet again, doing what he loved, telling stories about himself!

There was one story in particular that I was fascinated to hear. Finally, he was ready to tell it. Before Dad got to his "white collar" prison in Florida after his conviction for tax evasion, he was held over in one of those detention centers for hardened criminals. His job was to work in the kitchen. The kitchen supervisor warned him, "You do not give anyone more than one hamburger. Ya hear?"

"All right," Dad replied.

"I'm serious," the supervisor said. "No one gets more than one hamburger."

"Got it."

The next day while Dad was serving hamburgers to the prison inmates, a huge hulk of a man approached him and said, "I want two hamburgers."

"I can only give you one," Dad explained.

The man leaned closer, getting right up in Dad's face. "I'm telling you, man, if you don't give me two hamburgers, I'm gonna fuck you up."

Dad looked at the kitchen door and saw the supervisor who had told him, "Don't give anyone more than one hamburger."

The big man got even closer with his foul, rotten breath and warned, "You can't do that to me! You hear me? If you're not gonna give me two hamburgers, I wanna see you at 11:00 a.m. sharp in the hallway in Section C." Then he turned and stormed away.

Dad continued serving hamburgers—one only to each inmate, but he said he was scared.

Dean, an Irish guy, was in prison at this same time. The rumor was that Dean was a hitman, but he did eventually get out of prison, so he must not have been in for murder (at least not then!). Dean was

The Princess of 42nd Street

standing behind this great big guy, listening. And he knew this man had hurt people badly in this prison.

When Dean reached the front of the line, he told Dad, "Marty, this guy is a tough motherfucker and has hurt a lot of men in here. You could be killed. Just listen to me and do as I say." Dad was pretty scared, so he paid attention.

Guys often made makeshift knives, also known as shivs, in prison. Dean and another guy, we'll call him Steve, got together some shivs and went to this meeting with Daddy, planning to protect him and themselves. They arrived in Section C at 11:00 a.m. sharp.

When the huge hulk of a man showed up, Dean and Steve rushed him, shoving their shivs into the big man's side. They didn't really hurt him, they just stuck the shiv in far enough to let him know they meant business.

"Listen!" Dean screamed at him. "Marty doesn't know who the fuck you are. He just got here two days ago. But he'll give you all his cigarettes." (Cigarettes were the main currency in jail.) "Do you understand, big guy, who you're messing with?"

The man, who was twice Dean's size, nodded.

"This big guy knew who Dean was connected to," Dad explained. "And after that, the big guy let me go. Dean saved my life, to tell you the truth."

Dad laughed as he told Risa and me this story. Dean turned out to be one of the members of the ultra-violent Irish mob known as "The Westies," and when Dad got out of jail, these guys protected him. Dad said the leader of the group would beat up men who owed him money. Dad had a great idea and said to the leader, "Let them work for me so they can pay you back." And that relationship turned out to be one of the best things that could have happened to Dad. In fact, Dean was one of those guys who used to come to the house, and Dad would warn him not to stare at my boobs!

I remembered that once Dean was out of prison, he came to a lot of parties at our house. "Dean was a good friend to you, wasn't he?" I remarked.

"Yeah, he was," said Dad. "Sure had some good times with Dean." Risa knew Dean too and she also liked him. It's really weird how killers can be surprisingly nice guys.

After telling us a few more stories, it was obvious that Dad was getting very tired and I nodded to Risa that we should go. We tried to help him up but he looked at me like I was nuts—he would do it himself.

As we stood at the door and said goodbye, both Risa and I added in unison, "Love you, Daddy."

He looked at us both with his muddy-brown, watery eyes and I caught a flicker of emotion, flaring briefly like a match before winking out.

"Love you too, girls," he wheezed as he turned slowly and struggled to take the few steps back into the kitchen.

As we closed the door and walked down the hallway to the elevator, reality hit me hard, like a knife to my soul, and I told Risa, "This is it. Ris...you must get ready for the end... Daddy never says he loves me."

When Risa and I left our father that day, the last day we ever saw him alive, I felt such deep sorrow, it was hard to breathe at times. I was so scared of losing my father. From someplace deep inside me, I was already grieving for a love that had long been lost. I was so upset I could never get close to him. So upset he never told me he was proud of me. And now it was too late.

"When are you going to get a real job?!" he would say to me at times.

"You must be kidding me!" I always shot back. "I have had my own business for years!" As mentioned earlier, I sold to the natural food industry for 22 years. I was one of the first female brokers in the industry and actually helped build the industry from Maine to Pennsylvania. I trained reps and buyers in the stores, dealt with 24 manufactures at one time and held trainings for my buyers at the Plaza and the Waldorf.

Even so, none of that was good enough for Dad. He would goad my third husband, Edward, saying, "Eddie, is she really makin' any money? C'mon? *She* makes money?" Eddie was so close to his own mother and father and could not fathom the things he saw my father doing to me and my siblings. But one thing is certain to me now, learning to take care of myself financially was one of the best gifts I could ever have given myself.

But then again, there would be times when I was at his house and I would open his kitchen cabinets and see all the herbs I had suggested he try. This, to me, was my validation that he did in fact respect and admire what I was doing, even if he couldn't tell me so myself.

Good-bye, Daddy, I thought to myself as Risa and I walked to our car that terrible day of our final visit. *Godspeed and take care. May you find peace.*

Dad was laid to rest on Tuesday, May 27th, three days after he died, at the Riverside-Nassau North Chapel on Long Island. About 60 people attended and most were friends of Dad and Andrea. None of Dad's extended family was there—they'd stopped being involved with us many years ago, and I felt we had no one to turn to.

At the funeral, I walked around in shock. I couldn't talk. The whole environment seemed so surreal, with nothing tangible that I could wrap my heart around. Being the oldest of my siblings, I always felt a responsibility for everyone and everything, including my dysfunctional parents. But Dad's death made me feel helpless.

The casket was open during the viewing and everybody was going up to see my father, oohhhing and ahhhing and commenting on how great he looked in his $1,500 suit.

"Look at my Hody! Doesn't he look fantastic?" Andrea pranced about, talking about spending $30,000 of Dad's money on his funeral, acting like she was at a party. "Oh, hello, how are you?" "Don't you look nice!" "How have you been?"

I wanted to choke her. Strangle her. Tear her eyes out. *How could she behave like this is her birthday party?* Some people might say she was in shock, but from our experience this was just how she rolled. Money and things are everything to her.

We all knew this when she would come up to us at a dinner and push her wrist in our faces and say, "Look what your faaather bought me!!"

I always wanted to say, "Now we all know you caught him cheating on you. Terrific, Andrea...another bauble for you." He always had to buy her something very expensive when he got caught cheating...suffice it to say, her closet must have been like a jewelry store.

Risa and I talked for a bit and I told her, "I don't know how much longer I can stay here. I'm going to be sick if I have to be around Andrea any longer."

"I know," Risa said. "But we have to stay until they close the casket."

I heard someone, I don't remember if it was Andrea or Risa, but they both agreed Dad didn't have his glasses on and didn't look like himself. So they found the glasses and put them on Dad, eliciting a new round of ooohs and aaahs about how terrific he looked.

I never went up to see him. I just couldn't.

When they called for the casket closing, I felt physically ill. What could I do? I looked through the doorway into the chapel and could see the right side of his head, with his glasses and his gray hair and I just lost it. I walked to the railing of the stairs and just broke down, releasing the sobs that shook my chest and burned my lungs. No more Marty. Shit. No more heartache, no more listening to his stories, no more hurting me and my siblings. Even though he was so often cruel, he was also full of life. But now, that life was over.

We still had to endure the party afterward at the restaurant at the North Shore Towers. This was the first time I saw my nephews, Ben and Daniel, in many years after my sister Rhonda and I had a terrible misunderstanding. I was amazed how tall both boys had become. And Ben with a girlfriend! Daniel had a girlfriend too, but for some reason she was not able to come.

Andrea's two daughters were at the party. I had tried to be friendly with them, but as I mentioned earlier, Andrea took care of that. Anyway, after a while I heard some arguing. These girls had known my father in a different way than we did. They had known him since they were around seven and nine, I believe. They had a deadbeat dad and my father was good to them. I was happy for them. But don't tell me how I should feel about my father. Don't tell me or my siblings how great he was to us and that we shouldn't complain.

This was not the place to get into that, but then Andrea started screaming, "Get his kids away from me! I don't want them around me!" I had come in at the end and just heard the younger daughter saying how "lucky" we were and I yanked Risa and Rhonda away. "Not here!" I said. "We just buried Dad!"

"It just happened," one of them tried to explain.

Andrea walked away screaming with her girls behind her, and this was our chance to leave. She was still screaming at us to get away from her. We were fucked and we knew it. There was no way she was going to make anything easy for us.

I remember when I first met her, I was so happy. I thought, as we all did, "Wow, maybe she will be like a mother to us!" I was filled with hope. But that didn't last long. I don't remember if it was our first dinner together, but close. We were at a restaurant and I was in the bathroom stall when I heard someone come in.

"Where are you!!??" she slurred. She was drunk and who knows what else.

"Andrea?" I said, surprised.

She started pounding on the door of the stall. "Open this door!" she demanded.

What the fuck? "Wait a minute," I said as I pulled up my panties.

I opened the door and she closed it, leaned against the wall and started to slide down the wall. "You are taking MMMYYYY money!" she wailed as she plopped onto the dirty floor.

Holy shit, we are fucked! I said to myself. "Andrea, please, don't worry, there is plenty of money for everyone." *So much for my new mommy.*

That is my enduring memory of Andrea. I hope she is happy with what she's done.

When it was finally time to leave the party after the funeral, Risa came over to me and put her arm around my shoulder, giving me a warm, loving hug.

"You know what, Risa, all the torture is over now," I told her. "No more Dad or Mom to hurt us anymore."

She smiled. "But at least we've got each other," she said softly. I knew that hell was about to break loose in the coming weeks and months. Even though Dad was worth millions, we weren't sure if he had left anything for us kids like he had promised. Andrea had shown us how interested she was in Dad's money, and we all knew that we were in trouble now that Dad had died first.

Fuck it, I thought. *Fuck Andrea. I'm a survivor. I've survived so much crap in my life, I'll get through this just like I've gotten through everything else.* And then I spared a thought for Dad, with his soul still on its journey to the other side. *Thank you, Dad, for everything. I owe much of my strength to you, to having been your daughter. What a crazy, wild ride we had.*

Epilogue

The Princess of 42nd Street: The Journey Continues
Summer 2018

Well, it looks like I made it! I've survived the crazy ride that has been my life so far. What an extraordinary journey it has been, and in my mind, the journey is far from over. At age 61, (Thank God the new 61 still looks like 45... well, maybe 50!) I am convinced my best years are still ahead of me, and I can't wait to see what's next.

Today, I am happier than I've ever been, in great health, and splitting my time between Boynton Beach, Florida, and my cozy cottage in Wading River, Long Island. Having finished writing this book, I'm working on the sequel—because I believe you'll want to know a lot more about all the joys and challenges I experienced from 1982 to 2018!

I'm also busy building a new business, "Creating Harmony," in which I help people create a balanced and healthy relationship with alcohol through the principles of MM—Moderation Management. Not everyone who drinks too much is an alcoholic; in fact, there are many more problem drinkers than alcoholics in the world. Many of us just need to learn how to consume alcohol more responsibly. I help these people, based on my own history of problem drinking.

I have been working with the tools of MM for more than 12 years, leading groups in Manhattan, Long Island and here in Florida. The program has saved my life and many others. Many clients desire anonymity or to connect from the comfort of their office or home, so we connect online over Zoom. My goal is to offer tools and support, guiding people to create a new relationship with their drinking. Some clients even become leaders, and then go on to start groups of their own.

At the same time, I am also expanding my work as an inspirational public speaker, sharing my personal story of overcoming obstacles and helping others apply what I've learned from my experiences to their own situations and concerns. My ultimate goal is to work with men and women, especially women, those who have been abused, and at-risk teens. This kind of work can be really challenging, of course, but so deeply fulfilling as well. Helping people learn how to feel better about themselves and their circumstances makes me know my life has meaning, and all the pain and suffering of my past is not in vain.

I wish I could tell you that all the relationships within and among my family members have been healed, but unfortunately, that's not the case. But we're working on it, and we will continue working on it as long as we need to. After all, our parents gave us a lot to overcome! The legal issues surrounding my dad's estate and his widow, Andrea, are still working their way through the courts and probably will for some time.

Risa and I, after some very rough patches, are closer now than ever before. And Rhonda? Well, we haven't quite mended our fences yet, but I love her very much, and I miss my nephews, Ben and Daniel, terribly, along with her husband, Alan. She lucked out with him. My younger brother, Jarrett, is doing as well as can be expected after the devastating accident that changed his life forever, and every time I visit him, I can still see and feel the kind, loving, funny, mischievous man he was and always will be. And thank you to his wife, Toi... for keeping him alive and happy.

I'm not in a romantic relationship at the moment, but I'm actively dating, and actively anticipating the arrival of the loving partner with whom I am destined to share the rest of my life. Mr. Right, would you please HURRY up and get here, dammit!?! We've both got a lot of great memories we need to start making together!

I can't honestly say that I'm fully healed from all the trauma I've experienced, but I have made, and I'm making, tremendous progress. For so much of my life, I was completely detached from my feelings—blank, numb, dissociated, a typical coping mechanism among those who have been traumatized and abused. I remember one of my many therapists looking at me during one particularly challenging session and saying, "Romola, come back into your body now."

I gazed at her and thought, "What the fuck is she talking about? Where else could I be besides inside my body?" But now that I'm further along my journey and have had more healing, I understand what she meant, and I now allow myself to feel the full range of my emotions, from the highest highs to the lowest lows. This can be a terrifying process, but so very important for a healthy life. It is liberating to overcome trauma and learn to be more peaceful and kind to yourself inside because, as they say, it is an inside job. (Then again, a good Grey Goose martini never hurts!)

When I look back on my journey, especially when I recall myself as a kid, I wonder how I ever had such determination, or found such strength to stand up to my parents when they hurt me or my siblings. Where did that *chutzpah* come from? When I first started writing my story several years ago, I had a writing teacher questioning whether I was remembering it accurately, asking if I was "sure" I had spoken to my parents the way I described, or if I had "really" wrestled the wooden spoon out of my mother's hand at such a young age, hitting her with it when she threatened to hurt me. Had I really been so brave, so fearless? Yes, it really happened that way, but it wasn't only bravery that drove me, it was a deep-seated sense of right and wrong.

I believe that I was born with this commitment to fairness and a need to stand up for others who don't have a voice. I remember the strength it took to knock on my mother's bedroom door to ask for money for the kids for school, or to muster the strength to tell my father to leave the kids or Mom alone when he was lashing out at them, verbally and physically. My perspective was one of, "I don't give a shit what happens to me—I can handle it. I will take the pain so they don't have to." This has been my mantra for as long as I can remember.

I always believed that I was an "old soul" and told myself, "I am going to be Romola Hodas just this one time, I'll only visit earth once in her skin, so I have to find out what makes me happy and then never stop going for it, no matter what." For me, the answers to my questions came through learning to talk to myself kindly and with compassion. I know I will make mistakes, so I acknowledge them and move on. I ask forgiveness from myself and others and push forward, never doubting that I am a good person at heart.

Reaching this point in my journey has not been easy. For a long time, I thought, because I had been in therapy for so much of my life, that I would be "cured" one day. But not too long ago, I found out that this is not true, and that I will always be affected by my childhood; I'll always be challenged in some way by the things I experienced.

"What the hell? You mean this doesn't ever go away?" I said to my therapist, stunned. I cried really hard that day, having to accept that I will always carry inside me these feelings of not being good enough. But I have made such progress toward the goal of accepting that I am human, and we all have our moments of doubting ourselves. So we must remember to have gratitude for who we are and be in gratitude for all we have.

Being in and out of therapy for so long has helped me immensely. Finding the right therapist is very important. I know, because I have had some doozies! It's a never-ending discovery to gain more self-acceptance, to know I am fine the way I am, but I still want to keep growing and evolving, continuing on my journey to learn how to be happy, in this body, with me.

I have found it extremely valuable to find and connect with mentors, whether in person or on the internet, wise teachers who could help guide me on my journey. When I was utterly broke and deeply depressed, I found hope, help and healing with Esther Hicks, Linda Hall, Eckhardt Tolle, Oprah Winfrey, Deepak Chopra, and others, whom I listened to every day on my laptop and who helped me change my pattern of thinking. I listened to CDs and practiced self-hypnosis to generate positive energy, combat depression, moderate my drinking, etc. I also blast my favorite music and dance my ass off. Thank you Grateful Dead, Dave Matthews Band, U2, REM, The Cure, Florence and the Machine, Michael Jackson, and so many more. Music is a sure way to get me feeling better and remind me that there is joy in the world.

I knew even as a child that I didn't want to have children, and that's a decision I've never regretted. I did something very smart when I was about 15. I decided to talk to all of the mothers I knew and explained I was doing a poll and would they be as honest as they could. Don't you know that all of them said they loved their children, but if they knew then what they knew now, they wouldn't have done it. All of them. I took that seriously and I made up my mind.

I felt I was like a wild horse; I wanted to be free and see the world. I wanted to marry, and my husband and I would be the best of friends. All the problems of children would not come between us. I knew back then that if two people didn't have the same views on how to bring up their kids, it would be pure hell. I would have wanted to make sure that no one ever messed with my kids. I watched what happened between me, my siblings and my parents, and I couldn't bear to see that happen to children of my own.

Even though I've never given birth, I have nurtured many people throughout my life. From taking care of my younger siblings when I was just a kid myself, to caring for my teenage nieces when Risa wasn't able to, to my many friends, the men in my life, my colleagues and manufacturers in the natural food industry, and even now with the people whom I help moderate their drinking. As women, we have so much maternal energy that we can use to help other people so far beyond those we just happen to carry in our wombs and give birth to.

Thank God, through my nurturing and caregiving, I have learned to take care of myself first, before anyone else. (Most of the time, anyway—no one is perfect!) Perhaps it's becoming cliched to say it, but like they tell you during the safety instructions on an airplane, when the oxygen masks drop down, you have to put your own on first and make sure it's secure and working before you can help any of the people around you.

This focus on self-care has been especially important during the past 14 years which, as you'll read in this book's sequel, was a period almost as rough as my childhood. Too much happened to be able to do it justice here in a short summary, but some of the "highlights" of those 14 years include a controlling husband, a third divorce and losing my ex's family that I loved as my own, further family estrangement, Risa almost dying from a drug overdose and me having to take in her daughters when I had no money to support them, a backstabbing partner and my business destroyed after 22 years, a second business destroyed in Hurricane Sandy, bankruptcy, homelessness, my best buddy, Ray, dying after a 30-year friendship, and the death of my brother-in-law Alex, not to mention Jarrett's accident and the deaths of both my parents.

The only way I survived these nightmares was by trying to be kind to myself, nurturing the hurt little girl who still lives inside me.

Confident that I will live to 96, I was bound to have some hard years. Who the hell knew they would last over a decade! Sometimes I couldn't find the right attitude and it was hell. But I never stopped putting one foot in front of the other and believing in myself and the universe. When things were at their worst, extra support came from a man named Michael who brought me back to life. Boy, did he bring me joy!

I've long been a believer in the so-called "Law of Attraction," which, according to the website www.thelawofattraction.com, "is the ability to attract into our lives whatever we are focusing on... It is the Law of Attraction which uses the power of the mind to translate whatever is in our thoughts and materialize them into reality." In other words, if we learn to put a positive spin on the things that happen in our daily lives, positive things will be drawn to us. And if we bog down our minds with negative chatter, then we invoke negative energy and more of the same is created.

This is not to say that we sit on our asses and just think good things. We need to be an active participant in our own journey. Moreover, we are responsible for everything that happens in our lives, everything that affects us, good or bad. And of course we will have negative thoughts, but it is becoming aware of them and discovering new ways of thinking that helps us create a better life. Never judge yourself if you are experiencing negative emotions... just focus on changing them.

Even though I am a follower of the Law of Attraction, this created some conflicts and confusion for me when I considered my own journey. Certainly I didn't "choose" to be born the daughter of the Porno King and his mentally ill wife, nor did I choose to be abused. I didn't ask to be almost kidnapped or sent to reform school. No one would have wanted to grow up surrounded by the violence, chaos, and depravity I constantly found myself trying to navigate. But, if my own thoughts had created my circumstances, then wasn't I personally responsible for all the pain and suffering I had endured? This thought troubled me greatly.

Fortunately, I went to see Nicole, a clairvoyant. I asked her about this and she said, "Romola, you are so strong. You are a healer. There is nothing wrong with you. You didn't 'choose' or attract the terrible things that have happened to you. Quite the contrary: you were placed into this life for a reason, and that reason is to help your family and the other people around you. Your 'choice' was to be here to help them. Your mission was to be strong and protect them, and you have succeeded."

For me, this conversation was a life-changer (thank you, Nicole!), and helped guide me from thinking that even with all the hard work I was doing on myself, I must still be harboring some seriously defective energy somewhere. Nicole helped me to see that I am strong, loving, kind, intelligent, and pretty… (yeah, pretty!) I have the strength to be there for others and for myself.

This has been really significant for me. I even put up flattering photos of myself all over my home so I can see and appreciate the woman I have become. A curvy girl, sure, but no more Fat Moley for me! This might sound strange to some people, but on days I feel fat and ugly, I just look at the photos and say, "Remember who you are, Romola."

When I'm in New York, I'll occasionally stop by 42nd Street, the King of Porn's old haunting ground, and I barely recognize the place that played such a huge role in shaping me and my life. Gone are the pimps and whores, the junkies shooting up in doorways, the gutters full of trash, the XXX theaters with their garish marquees, replaced now by the stalwarts of slick, clean corporate America: McDonalds, Bank of America, Ruby Tuesday, Hard Rock Café. If Marty Hodas's influence is still here, it's faint, and fading, a ghost rattling its chains, a whisper on the wind on warm, summer nights.

In closing, I see my future so clearly. At last I can say that I am following my dream to help people learn to moderate their drinking using Moderation Management tools. I look forward to helping young adults learn to choose themselves and always talk kindly to themselves. And I have finally told my family's story, warts and all. In short, I am thrilled to announce that the Princess of 42nd Street is well on her way to finding inner peace, love, happiness and a bunch of fun at last!

Acknowledgments

There are so many people I would like to acknowledge. People who have been in my life at different times and who taught me things and then moved on. People who stayed through the years. People I am just meeting. Let me start:

To my father... thank God I inherited your energy, motivation, persistence and charisma. Mom, thank you for the moments you were soft and creative. Thank you for giving me such a healthy, positive attitude toward sex. I imagine things being much better for you up there.

To my sisters, Risa and Rhonda... thank you for the journey and the lessons. Ris, thanks for letting me live with you when I had no place else, even though it was really hard. And thank you for going through all that hell with me and coming out on the other side. Thank you for finally saying you understand me. Jarrett, my dear baby brother, you have made me laugh and made me cry. I don't think I ever met a person who didn't like you. Even now, with all you have gone through, and are still going through, your soul shines through and you make me laugh. Toi, what can I say? You saved my brother's life, and you can cook for me anytime! I love you.

Thank you, Steven, the best lawyer! Todd, thank you for listening to me for what seemed hours and making me feel heard. Marc, thank you for watching out for Jarrett and Toi. Thank you Santoh...

Thank you, Veronica, my angel niece; boy, we have been through an amazing ride. I am so proud of you. I am enjoying watching you grow. You have become an amazing young woman. I can't wait to see the life you create, and we need to travel more together! Leyna, I wish everything good for you and hope you find it in your heart to know I did the best I could. Alan, I love you. Daniel and Ben, I miss you more than you know. Please remember the good times, and I hope you come back into my life. I love you both. Izzy, you're like an uncle to me. You're family.

To Laurel, Jolene, Karen, Jimmy, Wesley, Vicki, Anna, Beth,

Debbie, Cindy, and the Lynches. To Yvonne and Holly. The two Susans and David. And to Timmy and Billy. To my third-grade teacher. Thank you, Malverne.

To Caren Safarin from Napanoch... forgive me for freaking you out in Brooklyn. I was young... would love to hear from you. To Knuckles. I have been looking for you since I left my first marriage...wondering if you are still alive; thank you for amazing memories—call me. Thank you, Earl, Cary, Brian and you, Joey... you saved my life for a while and gave me joy. You taught me about love and had me traveling America. I still have the pictures. And all the different bootlegs of the Dead! Thank you to Joey's family, some with whom I am still in touch.

To Stacey, Jo, Debbie, Pam, Ronnie, Linda, Joni, Alida... thank you for making me feel that some people were there for me. I know there were others but I don't remember all the names. Thank you to Lawrence, Long Island. To the girls in college who stuck up for me...thank you so much!

To Barry, my feng shui teacher, thank you for all those hours, for your concern, and for teaching me magic. I appreciate all you did.

Thanks, Grandma Mina, for showing me so much love. Kenny, Lynne, Jay, Gordon, Russell and Kevin... wish we could have known each other better. To my long-lost cousin Ronnie and your mom, too... so glad we have connected again and thanks for the help with my dad's family history. To Aunt Elaine—I wish things could have been easier for you.

To the girls and staff, especially McFoo, from the START Center... I hope you have moved forward and life is all that you want. To Karen... thank you for making me feel safe back then and wishing you much success going forward. Cathy, I hope you are well. Where are you?

To Bob... my dear friend. Thank you for all the wonderful times and still being there. Thank you for getting Joey to listen to something other than the Grateful Dead sometimes!! To Susan... I wish it didn't turn out this way. Sara and Bobbi...I love you. Marybeth, I hope you look down on me sometimes. Kitty...thank you for many years, even if they were hard for you.

Thank you, Eric, and all my comrades from MM! You saved my life.

Carla, you were my rep up in New England for Harmony Marketing.

You have become another important person in my life. Thank you so much for your friendship. I love you.

Gibby... I hope you are well.

Carlos...Thank you for sending my life in the amazing direction you did, introducing me to essential oils, the body-mind connection, Puerto Rico, vegetarianism, your mother and crispy rice from the bottom of the pan. Thank you for being one of the kindest, gentlest, most loving souls. I am glad you are still in my life.

Billy, what to say...you are a fun, crazy man... who made me feel like Marilyn Monroe...and boy, did I need that. Thank you.

Edward... my dear Edik. I thought we would be together forever. I want to thank you for how you took care of me through our divorce and after. I wish you and your family everything good. Marina and Ruslan... I am glad you were in my life and gave me a family. Katia...I miss you so much. Momma and Papa... you will never know how much you meant to me. You were absolutely the parents I never had. I miss you so. And I thank you so much for teaching me how to pick mushrooms and for loving me so. Lithuania was one of the most magical times of my life.

Rosemary, Jeff, Jessica, Billy, Andrew, Lena, Aunt Linda and Bobby. You also gave me, and Risa, too, a family that we so needed. We probably never would have been friends if not for Ray. Thank you for being there. We really miss your holiday dinners.

Ray... my best buddy. I miss you so. Remember when we were at the convention and it was you and me on the dance floor? Everyone moved out of the way to let us dance. Boy, we had fun. You were my first account in the natural food industry, and all the brokers loved you, too. You were my brother, lover and friend. You were the best, always there...always. My mother loved you and Dad called you Tatootels... I feel you watching me sometimes... please come visit... but just in the daytime.

Michael... what can I say about you? You brought me back to life when it was almost the worst I ever knew. I lost my business, my marriage, my husband's family, went bankrupt, my brother got hurt... and so much more. I couldn't move, and then there you were... putting life back into my veins. I miss being on your motorcycle, listening to your stories, South Hampton, West Palm Beach, and just watching you talk, cook breakfast and your amazing bed...

Rachael... my Rachael. I know from you that I can be young forever. I know from you how to live simpler. I know from you how to laugh my ass off...drink and be merry...swim in ice water and enjoy a woman I never would have been friends with, because you are my neighbor in Wading River, I lucked out. I love you.

Thanks, Datcha! My cottage on the north tail of Long Island. And to Eddie Hulse...who, when I was on my knees, let me skip my payments. I promised him I wouldn't say how long he let me go without paying! God bless you...and Astrid. To all the people at Hulse Camp. Thank you for being friendly...even though you think I am so strange.

To Marie Suk for helping me heal. To Dr. Rubin...I miss you. Dr. Schwartz...I hope you are showing more integrity. To Bonnie, my first alternative counselor. To Gracia and Debbie from Queens Counseling—thank you for helping me through a freakin' hard time. To the natural food industry for helping me become the woman I am. Thank you, Cindy, and your husband, Doug. We did have some great times building the industry. Thank you, Nancy, for all of our talks. I am sorry, Irena... I miss you.

Thank you, Gundi. The women's group was great that year. Although A. was so disappointing and hurtful.

To the women I am meeting here in Florida. Thank you for opening your hearts to me and being involved in my new journey.

To Laura... my guardian angel. You don't know what your friendship is doing for me.

To David and Marsha. Life is so much better with you as neighbors!

To Natalie and Don, my dear friends. Natalie, your patience with me as I learned the computer was out of this world. I never knew someone could be so kind. I am so happy we have developed such an amazing friendship. I am so happy both of you are in my life. Natalie, the book cover is awesome—thank you.

Sammy and Boots... I miss you. Sophie, I still can't believe it. Midget... I miss you.
Joni...through it all, we are still friends...someone I can be myself with always. I love you. Hannah...you, too, have been one of the best friends a person could ask for. Diane, my dear friend... may we go on forever laughing and being there for each other always.

And Liz. Elizabeth... mischievous and a heartbreaker. I have known you since we were 13. You were there in school when I

The Princess of 42nd Street

needed you so many times. And in adulthood. When my mother was dying and Jarrett got hurt. I can't even say we are friends—we are sisters. A rocky relationship for sure. I only want the best for you, and I hope you want that for me. Ken, thank you for being there so many times. AJ and Kim...you are family to me; I am always here for you. Proud of you both.

To my father's second wife. Are you happy with all the money? Many times, you said to us that money is the most important thing in life. Still think so? To Shari and Heather, I really tried to get close to you. She wouldn't have it. And we are hoping you will give us back our mother's jewelry when you get it.

Thank you, Lori Perkins, my publisher at Riverdale Avenue Books, and Alyssa Tognetti, my publicist. Thank you, Dan Gerstein from Gotham Ghostwriters. Thank you, Albert from Simba. Thank you, Mahesh Grossman of The Authors Team, for putting me in touch with Elizabeth Ridley. The book wouldn't exist without her.

Thank you, Steve Harrison and the whole crew at the National Publicity Summit and Quantum Leap. My new career will have much to do with you.

To Altichik, my hairy, four-legged son...you better be around another 15 years! I love you so much; you bring me joy.

Elizabeth Ridley. My co-author, my friend. I had a dream a long time ago, and you are helping it come true. I never, ever could have done this by myself. You keep me on course, you make me feel safe. You put everything together in a way I could not. It will be a sad time when 11:00 a.m. comes around and I am not talking to you on the phone. The summit was amazing! We co-created together and did a damn good job! I love you.

If I have missed anyone, I am sorry...didn't want this to go on for 20 pages. I owe my journey to all who have come into my path. Thank you. And to the love of my life who is out there somewhere... hurry to me soon!

--Romola Hodas,
Summer 2018

Resources

Learn More About This Book

The Princess of 42nd Street: Surviving My Childhood as the Daughter of Times Square's King of Porn www.theprincessof42ndstreet.com

Rialto Report (Podcast interview with Marty Hodas) https://www.therialtoreport.com/2014/06/29/marty-hodas-king-of-the-peeps-podcast-38/

Riverdale Avenue Books
http://riverdaleavebooks.com/

Learn More About Romola

Creating Harmony
https://www.creatingharmonymm.com/

Moderation Management
https://www.moderation.org/

To Get Help for Abuse and Mental Illness

National Center for Missing and Exploited Children
http://www.missingkids.com/home
NAMI: National Alliance on Mental Illness
https://www.nami.org/

About the Authors

Romola Hodas was born in Queens and raised on Long Island, the oldest of four children of a brilliant, bipolar mother and Times Square's notorious "King of the Peep Show" pornographer father Martin Hodas. She has survived and thrived after the violent, chaotic and unpredictable childhood detailed in her memoir.

Romola pursued a BA in psychology at the C. W. Post Campus of Long Island University in New York and has completed numerous health and wellness practitioner programs throughout her career. An accomplished and diversified entrepreneur and businesswoman, Romola has significant experience in public relations, marketing, advertising, human resources, community affairs, energy work and much more. She has developed and led corporate training programs and health awareness seminars for corporate staffs and other organizations.

For more than 20 years, Romola owned and operated Harmony Marketing, selling products to, and helping to grow, the natural food industry. She was one of the industry's first women to build her own business as a broker. Today she divides her time between Long Island, New York, and Boynton Beach, Florida, where she is building her new business, "Creating Harmony," working as a consultant, healer and public speaker.

Elizabeth Ridley is the author of five novels from major publishers, most recently *Searching for Celia* (Bold Strokes Books, 2015). In addition to *The Princess of 42nd Street: Surviving My Childhood as the Daughter of Times Square's King of Porn*, she is also the coauthor of three other memoirs: *Saving Sadie: How A Dog That No One Wanted Inspired the World* (with Joal Derse Dauer, Kensington/Citadel, 2017), *IncrediBull Stella: How the Love of a Pit Bull Rescued a Family* (with Marika Meeks, Kensington/Citadel, 2019) and *The Longest Battle: A Vietnam*

Vet Looks Back (with Tim Fortner, Texas Tech University Press, 2019). A recipient of both a Hawthornden Fellowship and a Literary Artist Fellowship from the Wisconsin Arts Board, she has a bachelor's degree in journalism from Northwestern University and a master's degree in creative writing from The University of East Anglia in Norwich, England, where she studied under former Poet Laureate Sir Andrew Motion. She lives in Milwaukee.

Other Riverdale Avenue Books Titles You Might Enjoy

A Star Shattered: The Rise and Fall and Rise of a Wrestling Diva
By Tamara "Sunny" Stych

We Love Jenni: The Unauthorized Biography of Jenni Rivera
By Marc Shapiro

*You're Gonna Make It After All:
The Life and Times and Influence of Mary Tyler Moore*
By Marc Shapiro

Annette Funicello: America's Sweetheart
By Marc Shapiro

*Welcome to Shondaland:
An Unauthorized Biography of Shonda Rhimes*
By Marc Shapiro

Made in the USA
Lexington, KY
30 September 2018